Early National Education, 1776-1830

Studies in the History of American Education Series

Henry J. Perkinson
and Vincent P. Lannie
General Editors

Sheldon Cohen
A History of Colonial Education, 1607–1776

David Madsen
Early National Education, 1776–1830

Frederick M. Binder
The Age of the Common School, 1830–1865

Patricia Albjerg Graham
Community and Class in American Education, 1865–1918

Edgar Gumbert and Joel H. Spring
The Superschool and the Superstate:
American Education in the Twentieth Century, 1918–1970

Early National Education: 1776-1830

David Madsen
University of Washington

John Wiley & Sons, Inc., New York · London · Sydney · Toronto

Library of Congress Cataloging in Publication Data:

Madsen, David.
    Early national education, 1776–1830.

    (Studies in the history of American education series)
    Bibliography: p.
    1. Education—United States—History. I. Title.

LA808.M33 1974   370'.973   73–22218
ISBN 0–471–56326–9
ISBN 0–471–56327–7 (pbk.)

Printed in the United States of America

10 9 8 7 6 5 4 3 2 1

series preface

This series provides new interpretations of American educational history based on the best recent scholarship. It contains five volumes that present, chronologically and topically, the history of American education from the beginning to the present day.

Each volume gives an original analysis and interpretation of the development of formal and informal agencies of education during a particular period.

Henry J. Perkinson

contents

Early National Education, 1776-1830

chapter one
events: 1776-1831

In 1776, political economist Adam Smith advanced a remarkably accurate prediction on the future of the United States of America.

The persons who now govern the resolutions of what they call their Continental Congress, feel in themselves at this moment a degree of importance which perhaps, the greatest subjects in Europe scarce feel. From shopkeepers, tradesmen, and attornies, they are become statesmen and legislators, and are employed in contriving a new form of government for an extensive empire, which, they flatter themselves, will become, and which, indeed, seems very likely to become one of the greatest and most formidable that ever was in the world.

No one would dispute that the United States is a formidable power today; if wealth and power determine greatness, then this nation is great; but that we as a people have lived up to the precepts set forth in those extraordinary documents written in the first flush of revolutionary fervor is, for some, a matter of debate. Nevertheless, it is the spirit behind those noble aspirations, a spirit demanding constant change and

3

improvement, that continues to challenge a progressive society. And certainly few can deny that dramatic changes have occurred in the past two centuries to alter the face of America and the lives of its people. The force of many of these changes was already being felt in the first half century of the republic, and it was strong enough to propel it from the brink of military and political disaster to the status of a nation to be reckoned with by the Old World powers.

Like all nations, the United States was from the outset beset by a variety of problems—political, social, religious, geographical, cultural, educational, and technological. Although we will be primarily concerned here with matters pertaining to educational thought and institutions, we must also explore the interaction of developments in these areas with changes that were occurring in all the other phases of American life in the early national period.

Of major importance, of course, was the unprecedented expansion of territory and population in this era. The 13 original colonies embarked upon statehood with a total population of about 3 million. By 1790, when the nation encompassed 888,811 square miles, its inhabitants numbered almost 4 million, most of them on farms and in small villages; only slightly more than 200,000 lived in towns of 2500 or larger. In 1830, near the end of the era, there were 24 states with a total area of 1,788,006 square miles and about 13 million inhabitants, over 2½ million of whom had made the difficult trek westward to push the borders beyond the mountains. The ratio of urban to rural dwellers had altered slightly, with 1 million in the larger towns and nearly 12 million still in the rural areas. And despite the phenomenal increase in land mass, the population per square mile had grown from 4.5 to 7.4 persons.

It is easy to cite statistics of this sort, harder to deal with the infinitude of problems engendered by such rapid growth and expansion. It soon became obvious that an answer must quickly be found to the question of whether so vast a land and so diverse a population could be governed under the republican form of government designed by delegates to the Constitutional Convention of 1787. At the beginning of the early national period the answer must have seemed somewhat equivocal; as the decades wore on, however, the political convictions of the Founding Fathers were to be resoundingly affirmed. Nonetheless, the task of governance would never be easy. In time, technological advances such as the telegraph and the railway facilitated communication and travel and brought about an influx of immigrants that swelled the population and formed the basis of a labor and consumer market so essential to the industrial revolution. And the problems of governing a democracy continued to grow.

This chapter will not analyze the complex forces that shaped the course of events in the early national period. Historians and other scholars have produced countless volumes on the founding of the American Republic and its growth; the years to come will see many more such treatises devoted to the circumstances and events that have made this country what it is.

From the experience of the past two centuries, however, it is clear that violent revolutions, set in motion to resolve one set of unbearable circumstances, inevitably create others often equally intolerable. The revolutionary who wishes to see his goals accomplished must recognize that the rhetoric of revolution is devoid of substance as guidance for a new nation; the hot-headed patriot must be succeeded by the clear-headed thinker, or chaos will ensue and the revolution will end, as it did in France, with the country in flames and the intellectuals powerless and mute. Fortunately for the Americans, their leaders were able to keep both their heads and their counsel.

The struggle against Britain had ended after the defeat of General Cornwallis by the combined American and French forces at Yorktown in 1781, but hostilities did not officially cease until the signing of the Treaty of Paris in 1783. The first attempt at governing the new nation was made under the Articles of Confederation, which gave the central government power to declare war and to make peace; to appoint diplomatic representatives; to regulate the value of money, borrow funds, and emit bills of credit; to raise armies and navies; to direct Indian affairs; to fix standards of weights and measures; and to establish a postal system. With tasks of this magnitude, it is incredible that the government was expected to function with neither an executive nor a judicial branch. Furthermore, the Articles could be amended only by the approval of Congress and ratification by each of the states. It was with such inadequate machinery that a vast and expanding nation was to be governed, a land inhabited, moreover, by a diverse population that frequently gave its loyalties to a region instead of to the central government. No wonder men as foresighted as George Washington feared that regional conflicts might one day erupt into permanent division or civil war.

It must be remembered that these arrangements were the work of intelligent men who had broken with one government by violent means over what they regarded as intolerable oppression; not surprisingly, they were reluctant to impose on themselves and their countrymen another government that possessed the same potential for repression as the one they had overthrown. Their attitude is understandable, but unfortunately its result was the Articles of Confederation with their severe drawbacks, the most important of which stemmed from the fact that the Continental Congress simply was not granted the power to govern. If a state wished to resist or to ignore laws passed by the Congress, there was no machinery by which to enforce its obedience.

Although Congress was a body empowered only to make recommendations, it was by no means impotent. For example, it enacted the Land Ordinance of 1785 and the Northwest Land Ordinance of 1787, which assured settlers in the Northwest Territory the privileges of statehood as soon as certain conditions had been met. The good sense behind this means of admitting states into the Union provided a solution to the assimilation of western lands that had eluded the British. The latter had made the mistake of regarding the settlers as perpetual "colonials" instead of granting them the status of potentially full-fledged members of the commonwealth.

Thus, while the government under the Articles of Confederation was not a complete failure, it was clear by 1786 that a stronger central authority was needed if the nation was to remain unified and to continue to prosper. This conviction led to the Annapolis Convention, attended by delegates from five states. Little was accomplished beyond the adoption of Alexander Hamilton's resolution calling for yet another convention to be held in Philadelphia in 1787.

When the delegates to the Philadelphia meeting convened in the summer of 1787, there were a number of notable absences, among them Patrick Henry, Samuel Adams, Thomas Paine, and Thomas Jefferson. However, many of the ablest of their countrymen were on hand, including George Washington, Roger Sherman, Benjamin Franklin, Elbridge Gerry, Edmund Randolph, Robert Morris, James Wilson, and John Rutledge. It is to these men, as well as to others who were not present, that the United States is indebted for a Constitution that still unifies and governs a nation of diverse regions and peoples.

There is a naive assumption that the Founding Fathers contemplated a pure form of democracy as the surest means of insuring that unity; this view is contradicted, however, by the many uncomplimentary references in their proceedings to what Elbridge Gerry of Massachusetts termed an "excess of democracy," and charged with responsibility for the difficulties the country was undergoing. Alexander Hamilton was even more scathing in his denunciation of democracy: "All communities," he asserted, "divide themselves into the few and the many. The first are the rich and well-born, the other the mass of the people [who] seldom judge or determine right."

With the Constitution as the supreme law of the land, the states found it much more difficult to enact laws that would nullify the intent of the federal government. The drafters of the Constitution thereby accomplished the surprising feat of reserving powers to the states while at the same time creating a stronger central government that could call directly on individual citizens for support through such means as taxes and military service. In short, a way had been found to make the whole greater than the sum of its parts while yet retaining the integrity of the parts.

Nevertheless, as remarkable as it was, the solution provided under the Constitution was by no means perfect. For years debates raged around the question of "states' rights," and even before the Civil War brought the matter to a head, the citizens of more than one state had flirted with the drastic step of secession. Carl Sandburg has described the situation consummately in his assertion that the War Between the States was fought over a verb: "Before the War, it was 'The United States *are*'; after the War, 'the United States *is*.'"

Certainly one of the tragic flaws in the Constitution was its failure to halt the slave trade; in fact, Congress was actually prohibited from banning the importation of slaves for another 20 years. With the following words, the deed was accomplished, and the kindest attempts to interpret the motives of the Constitution's authors will not diminish the enormity of the evil: "The Migration or Importation of such persons as any of the States now existing shall think proper to admit, shall not be prohibited by the Congress prior to the Year one thousand eight hundred and eight. . . ."

When it came time to ratify the Constitution, several states, among them New York, Virginia, and Massachusetts, recommended the addition of a Bill of Rights. Accordingly, the first Congress proposed 12 amendments, 10 of which were duly ratified by 1791. These amendments were modeled closely on the Declaration of Rights, written by George Mason and adopted by Virginia in 1776. Curiously enough, Mason had attended the Constitutional Convention in 1787, but was not among the 39 signers, partly because of his objection to the vesting of too much power in a central government, partly because of the absence of a bill of rights. Needless to say, Mason and the authors of other basic statements of human rights, such as the

Declaration of Independence, the first 10 Constitutional amendments, and certain articles in bills of rights adopted by the several states, were indebted to various documents that ensured freedom in the mother country, such as the Magna Carta extracted from King John at Runnymede in 1215, the Declaration of Rights produced in England in 1689 following the revolution of the previous year, and other writings on the importance of individual liberty.

The new republic was launched on its perilous voyage in 1789, with George Washington as president, assisted by a superb cabinet that utilized the talents of men such as Alexander Hamilton as Secretary of the Treasury and Thomas Jefferson as Secretary of State. Almost at once, however, the republican ship was in danger of foundering in the wake of turbulent European conflicts. Washington, whose warning on the dangers of entangling foreign alliances was to be recalled, in many cases to their sorrow, by generations of Americans, chose neutrality as the safest course for his young nation.

Neutrality in the matter of European wars was one thing; a more warlike stance was considered necessary in conflicts with the domestic Indian population, which fiercely resisted the encroachment of the settlers on their ancestral lands. Only after the defeat of a confederation of Indian nations by General "Mad Anthony" Wayne at the Battle of Fallen Timbers in 1794 and the signing of the Treaty of Greenville in 1795, under which the Indians bowed to the authority of the Americans instead of the British, did a period of relative peace ensue.

Washington's vice-president, John Adams, replaced his former chief as president in 1796, and guided his country through treacherous waters constantly troubled by foreign wars and their accompanying intrigues. Unfortunately for Adams, his administration must bear responsibility for the infamous Alien and Sedition Acts, four laws aimed at French citizens living in the United States and sympathetic to the cause of the Jeffersonian Republicans, at journalists who were openly critical of the Federalists, and at certain others who found fault with the president and members of his political party. Ten persons, all Republicans, were found guilty, fined, and imprisoned under the Sedition Act. Eventually, revulsion against these laws cost the Federalists much popular sympathy and prompted contravening statements, such as the Virginia and Kentucky Resolutions, from the pens of Thomas Jefferson and James Madison.

Adams' term in office, moreover, saw the signing of a treaty with France (the Convention of 1800) that had the effect of loosening ties that had linked the countries since the wartime treaty of 1778. Ironic, indeed, that laws aimed at citizens of France in the United States should be enacted (the Alien Acts) and a treaty struck to sever an "entangling alliance" with the very nation that had done the most to aid Americans in their struggle for independence against Great Britain. When Adams left office in 1801 to make way for his Republican successor, Thomas Jefferson, the last Federalist president departed.

Less than 3 years after assuming the presidency, Thomas Jefferson had negotiated the purchase of the Louisiana Territory from France for $15 million, and an enormous expanse of western land was brought within the boundaries of the United States. In May 1804, Meriwether Lewis and William Clark set out to explore the newly acquired lands; the following year they reached the headwaters of the Columbia River, and eventually stood on the very shores of the Pacific Ocean.

On the eastern coast, however, there was the continuing threat of involvement in the interminable European disputes, and in 1807, the Congress responded by passing the Embargo Acts, which forbade American vessels to sail from domestic to European ports. This early attempt to employ economic sanctions in order to bring the European powers to their senses surely ranks in idealism and in futility with the passage in later years of the Eighteenth (Prohibition) Amendment to the Constitution. Inevitably, the principal result of the Embargo was not the smothering of the flames of European war, but the destruction of American foreign commerce and a concomitant increase in all manner of smuggling and evasion.

American relations with Europe underwent little improvement when James Madison replaced Jefferson as president in 1809. By 1810, leaders in the United States felt there had been sufficient provocation on the part of both Britain and France to contemplate going to war with either nation. While war with neither was in our best interest, the demand for war had reached fever pitch by 1812, and despite the fact that indignities had been suffered at the hands of France, it was Britain, the old enemy, that aroused the greater animosity; moreover, there was added provocation in the foothold retained on the North American continent by Britain in Canada and by her ally, Spain, in Florida.

Many New Englanders opposed the ensuing war with Britain, declaring it to be both ruinous and unconstitutional, as well as unjustifiable. Certain Federalists from Massachusetts, Connecticut, and Rhode Island went so far as to flirt with treason at the Hartford, Connecticut convention in 1814–1815, when they voiced opposition to the war and drafted Constitutional amendments venting their objections to the war, to the policies of the Jeffersonian Republicans, and to activities of the others. The war came to an end, however, before conclusive action could be taken on either side.

The War of 1812 saw several American naval triumphs, but few notable land victories. Indeed, the British actually succeeded in penetrating the defenses of the capital and burning many public buildings in Washington, D.C. Popular acclaim for Andrew Jackson's victory at New Orleans was dampened by the tragic fact that the battle had been fought 2 weeks after hostilities had officially been brought to a close by the Treaty of Ghent.

After the War of 1812, Americans began to move west in greater and greater numbers, their ranks now swelled by immigrants who sought to replace the oppressiveness of their European existence with the promise of opportunity and prosperity in the New World. Cheap land was a strong inducement to men who had never before tilled their own acres.

The doubling of cotton exports immediately after the War of 1812 created a brisk demand for more slaves and for more acres on which to cultivate cotton. Political repercussions were inevitable, and in 1820 (James Monroe was in the White House) the Missouri Compromise was effected, under which Maine and Missouri were admitted to the Union, Maine as a "free" state, Missouri with no restrictions on slavery. Moreover, the terms of the compromise called for the admission of all future states north of latitude 36°30′ as free states. In 1822, a free black, Denmark Vesey, led a brief slave uprising in South Carolina, this one no more successful than the Virginia revolt under the slave, Gabriel, in 1800 or the rebellion led by Nat Turner in 1831.

Two events of note occurred in 1825: the completion of the Erie Canal and the founding of Jefferson's University of Virginia. John Quincy Adams served as president from 1824–1828, having been elected over Andrew Jackson. Four years later, however, Jackson won the presidency and Adams returned to a long and distinguished career in the House of Representatives.

The newspapers in the early national period titillated their readers with accounts of glory and defeat on the battlefield, disputes over tariffs, the rhetoric of political demagoguery, and the scandal, villainy, rapine, and murder that are staples of our public press to this day. But more and more, as a corollary to the more dramatic events of the age, came news of scientific innovation and technological advances. In 1830, for example, passengers were carried on a horse-drawn railway; in 1831, Cyrus McCormick tested his reaper near Steele's Tavern, Virginia. Eli Whitney's invention of the cotton gin and his employment of mass production techniques were unquestionably equal in significance to the more dramatic public events of the time, for while today's political victory may be overturned when next the public goes to the polls, the invention of a machine such as the steamboat, the cotton gin, and the reaper can have an incalculable and frequently irreversible effect on the daily life of the people.

The closing decades of the period were characterized also by ferment in intellectual and educational circles. Dozens of institutions of higher learning opened their doors, including the colleges and universities of Georgia, North Carolina, South Carolina, Virginia, Michigan, Nashville, Transylvania, West Point, Rensselaer Polytechnic Institute, and Union College.

Professorships of medicine were being established in the faculties of various American colleges, and Judge Tapping Reeve's law school was organized in Litchfield, Connecticut. The academies that came into being at this time, such as Phillips, Liberty Hall (North Carolina), and York, were the forerunners of the massive effort in secondary education to be undertaken in the twentieth century. At a more elementary level, the Sunday school movement was introduced in the United States, as was the Lancastrian or monitorial system of instructing large numbers of children, which enjoyed a brief period of popular acceptance.

In New York a free school society was formed to educate the children of the poor; in Switzerland a teachers' training institute was opened by Johann Pestalozzi that would in time influence most educators in the Western world. Noah Webster, Jedidiah Morse, and Samuel Goodrich were at work on textbooks that would instruct millions of American schoolchildren.

Meanwhile the arts were also experiencing a flurry of activity. The influential *North American Review* began publication, and in Philadelphia a Musical Fund Society was founded. Many American painters made the pilgrimage abroad to learn the art of portraiture in the British studio of the American expatriate painter, Benjamin West. Writers and novelists such as James Fenimore Cooper, Charles Brockden Brown, and Washington Irving were laying the groundwork for native American literature. In a more pragmatic vein, American housewives were devising their decorative and often abstract patterns for quilts, coverlets, rugs, and were producing needlework, knitting, and crocheting of increasing skill and complexity, while craftsmen and artisans were turning out furniture and household articles, all with a peculiarly American stamp.

To most Americans, the advances in science, education, and

technology carried with them the promise of a better future. In the late nineteenth century, historian Henry Adams was to question why the European immigrant became a different man when he stepped off the boat onto American shores. The answer is apparent to anyone who has had nothing and is suddenly confronted with the chance to acquire something of his own. In America this bounty might include large tracts of land for fields and orchards; with industry, he might add buildings and livestock, tools and machinery. For others, it was even more important to gain the right to practice their religion with a minimum of interference from the community or state, or to see his children educated far beyond his own level. Of such stuff were the dreams of the immigrant made, and often they turned out to have substance. "Progress," "rising expectations," "the desire for economic and social mobility," "a new deal," "freedom from want," and many other phrases bespeak the recognized opportunity to pursue a dream.

To the immigrant, the indentured servant, even the adventurer, then, the United States represented an opportunity to improve the quality of life, to acquire land, wealth, and an education, to achieve, perhaps, a higher station than that to which he could have aspired in the Old World. That these expectations were so often fulfilled only compounded the tragedy of those who were denied the chance to realize them. The American Indian could choose to join the white settler, to live with him in an uneasy peace, or to flee before the engulfing wave of westward migration. It was the latter path that was most often taken, as inevitably the tribes were pushed farther and farther west, or confined to smaller or less desirable reserves of land. To the Indian, it was as incomprehensible that one man might sell the land to another as that he might barter away the air or the water on which his life depended.

And while the United States emerged as the world's leading producer of cotton, the black slaves whose labor produced that staple were also faring badly. Although the importation of slaves had been banned, smuggling continued and the sale of slaves remained a lucrative business as Western lands were opened to the cultivation of cotton and tobacco. Unhappily, the laws circumscribing the existence of the slave and the black freeman alike grew ever stricter over the years; by the 1830s, in fact, it was, in some places, illegal even to teach a slave to read.

Unlike the Indian, the slave could not run, but must contrive to exist under a system that was at best paternalistic. Even for the blacks who were technically free, the dream of his white brethren was far from fulfillment. And for this lamentable breach of its vaunted egalitarianism, the United States would pay an incalculable price, the payment of which is being exacted to this day.

chapter two

chapter two

life: new england, middle states and south

I know no safe depository of the ultimate powers of the society but the people themselves; and if we think them not enlightened enough to exercise their control with a wholesome discretion, the remedy is not to take it from them, but to inform their discretion. Letter from Thomas Jefferson to William Charles Jarvis, September 28, 1820.

During those yeasty decades in American history known as the early national period—roughly from 1781–1830—the education of the young was seldom left solely to the agents of formal schooling. Too often mere survival depended on skills a child could learn only by working shoulder to shoulder with his elders. Despite the value placed on book learning, this portion of his education often had to give precedence to the acquisition of the crafts and trades so essential to an expanding frontier-oriented society.

Before we consider the forces that shaped the education of young Americans in the late eighteenth and early nineteenth centuries, we will attempt to recreate a sense of the life they knew—not a simple task for one whose experiences encompass the startling inventions of the twentieth century. Imagine forgoing the pleasure and convenience of hot water flowing at the turn of a tap, of the electric light bulb, and of the television screen; know, instead, the fireplace or the wood-burning stove as the only source of heat, and the flickering firelight, the whale-oil lamp, or the candle illuminating the evening's task or entertainment provided by the family storyteller or musician.

Then ponder the truism that electricity has exorcised more ghosts than all the shamans, sorcerers, and clergymen who ever lived. Indeed, we in the twentieth century who would attempt to understand the fears and delights of a child of that earlier time must allow all the ghosts to return to their haunts in forest shadows, in barn lofts, and stairwells. We must forget the automobile, the airplane, the subway, the bus, and the pervasive fumes of gasoline, as we imagine instead the smell of dung, wool, and wet horsehide. We must try to understand the frustrations and the satisfactions of working with oxen and horses, of caring for cows, pigs, and poultry, of making soap in a black iron kettle over an open fire, and of eating with wooden utensils from a wooden bowl.

We must try to comprehend some of the commonplace experiences of the time: what it was like to pick cotton all day, to chop the weeds away from tobacco plants under the hot southern sun, to live in a log cabin, to sail before the mast in a schooner bound for France, to live in a small town in a white house with an outhouse in back, to trudge along a dirt road ankle-deep in mud after a summer rainstorm, to ride in a horse-drawn buggy or sledge, to burn logs in a fireplace, to shuck corn, to thaw a frozen pump with a kettle of hot water, to butcher a pig, to hunt squirrel, to read the Bible, to work at a weaving machine in a cotton mill in Massachusetts or Rhode Island for 13 hours a day, to sail on a ship carrying ice from New England to the West Indies, to read an almanac, to sit in church twice on Sunday listening to sermons, to mend the family clothing in the evening by firelight, to hunt whales in the South Pacific, to head West in search of land and a new life, to sink a plowshare into the rich farm land of the Shenandoah Valley, to live in the cities of New York, Boston, Charleston, Philadelphia, or Baltimore, to churn butter or bake bread or run away to the North and a bit more freedom, to tally accounts in a merchant's office in New York, to pick apples in Connecticut, to sew a quilt in Virginia, to put up hay in Kentucky, to preach a sermon in South Carolina. And we must recall that our forefathers and their offspring still found time to kneel before a wrathful God and to brood at length on the uncertainties of this life and the hereafter.

It is sometimes difficult for a child of the urbanized and industrialized twentieth century to comprehend the degree to which agriculture and the values of an agrarian society dominated all aspects of life in early America. The shopkeepers and tradesmen of the villages and towns depended on the fruits of the soil, as did the merchants of the growing cities and seaports. Some, Thomas Jefferson among them, saw in the rural existence a state of virtue conducive to independence and self-fulfillment in contrast to the urban life, which led to corruption and decay, or at the very least, to political and social instability.

The effect of a predominantly agricultural society on the education—formal and otherwise—of the young was crucial indeed. For just as the prosperity of society as a whole rested on the products of the farmer's labor, his own welfare depended in large part on the work contributed by each member of his own family unit. Consequently, children were expected to share at an early age the duties and responsibilities of their elders. Childhood and adolescence were regarded as stages of development through which one progressed as quickly as possible in order to assume the status as well as the burdens of an adult. The best way to achieve adult standing was to demonstrate the ability to perform the work of a grown man or woman—or at least to acquit oneself honorably in the attempt. It was not unusual to see a boy or girl as young as eleven doing a job that placed a severe physical strain on growing bodies. Boys, for example, plowed the fields, cared for livestock, and cut wood at the side of their fathers and older brothers. The girls baked bread, sewed clothing, made candles, and tended younger siblings as well as the garden and the chickens; they often helped their brothers in the fields at planting, haying, and harvest times.

In such a society, the family constituted a cooperative whole in which the life of each member—parent or child—depended on the industry, the skill, and the judgment of all the others. To be sure, most parents recognized their children's needs as growing youngsters, but inevitably they came to regard them as co-workers who required only the seasoning of experience and the flowering of their strength to stand as equals in the struggle to subdue a wild land or build the family enterprise. The children saw in their parents models to be emulated, for above all they represented the adulthood to which every young person must aspire. And both parents and children searched constantly the face of nature, the Scriptures, and one another for the visible signs of the wishes of God in the affairs of men.

The population of the United States in the early national period was a diverse one that knew the varying conditions of wealth and poverty, of piety and unbelief, of contentment and despair. In 1830, as the era drew to a close, 1 million people inhabited the larger towns and cities while more than 11 million lived on farms and in small villages. Agriculture, to be sure, continued to dominate the daily affairs of men, yet there was tremendous variety to be found in an agrarian community that encompassed so many different geographical regions. In the North, stretched along the rugged coastline of New England, were tidy villages of white houses and church spires and rocky fields bounded by walls built without mortar from the stones thrown up by frost and plow to be hauled away by the farmer and his sons. Pennsylvania was home to many settlers from Germany who took pride in neat farms and orchards. In the South were Anglicans essaying a life of Old World elegance on plantations where slaves harvested the crops of tobacco and cotton. Inland lay the small farms and settlements of the Scots, the Irish, and the Scots-Irish. Besides the farmers and planters of these various regions, there were the men who owned the shops, the ships, the mills, and the forges—and some who owned nothing at all, such as the native Indian population, pushed relentlessly westward as the frontier expanded.

New England

New Englanders in the early national period saw few examples of extreme wealth or degrading poverty, with the possible exception, in the latter case, of the Indians who had been displaced by earlier settlers. Most people had some sort of habitation and a little land to till and to support some livestock: a cow, a few hogs, a horse, poultry, and sometimes a few sheep. If conditions became desperate, there was always the prospect of moving westward to seek one's fortune, a recourse open to all but the sick, the shiftless, and the timid.

Most New Englanders of the day had to be content with simple pleasures, simple comforts, and simple fare. Corn, squash, and other vegetables came from the garden, cured pork from the brine barrel or smokehouse. Housewives baked loaves of bread to toast or spread with freshly churned butter and made puddings of corn, flour, rice, or buckwheat. Clear water, sweet milk, and cider, and tea at least one meal a day sufficed as beverages; stronger drink was often available (too often, to judge from the frequent pulpit denunciations of intemperance) in the form of porter, ale, wine, and rum.

Visiting, with its opportunity to exchange "thought, affection, hospitability, and pleasure," was perhaps the most popular social activity; opportunities for conversation were always welcome—indeed, on the frontier and in the isolated villages it was essential to the sanity of the inhabitants. Other pastimes that enlivened an existence a cultivated European might have found dull were walking, riding, dancing, shooting at a mark, oratory, and debate. Serenading was common, and in winter, sleighing and ice-skating were favorite outdoor diversions.

Reading was enjoyed by those lucky enough to have access to the relatively few public libraries or to sizable private collections. The two staples of literary fare in most households were the Bible and the Almanac; these books and others, and a growing number of periodicals, provided a solace more benign than the strong spirits against which the preachers railed.

Towns in which an academy or a college were located enjoyed the fruits of the literary and debating societies—poetry readings, oratory, debates—and even the final examinations of students on graduation day, which were open to the public and enhanced by a parade. The less cosmopolitan did not scorn the rough-and-tumble fight, the rules of which forbade only the use of iron weapons.

Inevitably, the New Englanders became a seafaring people whose commerce was to take them to distant lands. In ships built of native raw materials, they sailed from the Atlantic ports to hunt whales for oil and seals and sea otter for their pelts, and they returned with holds filled with tea, sandalwood, and an infinite variety of precious cargo. In their small factories and shops, artisans and craftsmen turned out earthenware, window glass, pewter, leather goods, gunpowder, hats, snuff, cloth of cotton or wool, jewelry, spirits, furniture, carriages, and many other wares. Some of these products were for domestic consumption, but much was exported in addition to fish, raw lumber, whale oil, rum, cheese, shoes, cloth, and nails. Coastal as well as international trade was brisk, and the shipping industry would see even busier days in the 1830s and ensuing decades with the construction of the swift clipper ships, surely the most beautiful vessels ever seen under sail. Their very names match the grace and splendor of their design: *Flying Cloud, American Republic, Sea Witch, Southern Cross, Cutty Sark, Comet,* and *Thermopylae.* What a pity that at its zenith, sailing was doomed to give way so soon to steam.

Wealthy Bostonians of the day showed some pretensions to elegance in their dress, favoring short breeches buttoned at the knee, often topped by colored coats and ruffled shirts with white cravats.

Timothy Dwight has given us an appealing picture of New

Haven, Connecticut, his hometown for many years. The homes he described were neat and tidy, commonly built of wood and (especially after 1800) painted white, with a fence at the sides and front, and an outhouse in the back. Among the public landmarks were houses of worship for the Presbyterians, Episcopalians, and Methodists, an alms house, Yale College, a state and county house, a jail, and a large wharf. Manufacturers and merchants plied a trade in dry goods, grocery, hardware, glass and china, shoes and boots, books, furniture, and paper. Other firms included the 12 inns, business houses engaged in foreign commerce, the ship and tallow chandlers, the apothecary shops, and the local shipyard. The professions were represented by clergymen, lawyers, physicians, and a surgeon; the crafts were represented by 29 blacksmiths, a bell founder and two brass founders, seven goldsmiths, watchmakers, harness makers, cabinetmakers, tailors, stonecutters, papermakers, tinners, barbers, coopers, bakers, wheelrights, curriers, masons, carpenters and joiners, bookbinders, and butchers. Beef sold from 7 cents a pound to 10 cents a pound for the better cuts; pork, veal, mutton, lamb, and all manner of poultry, fish, and shellfish were available in the markets. Flour was sold by the barrel, rye by the bushel, and Indian corn, apples, cider, and firewood were offered for sale. Dwight, in his comment on the relative absence of crime, added drily that it was fortunate, in view of the fact that the "police of the town [are] far from being either vigorous or exact."

The life of the farmer was an arduous one, with 6 days a week devoted to the growing of maize, wheat, rye, barley, flax, buckwheat, oats, and hay. Although crop rotation and the use of manure as fertilizer were practiced to some extent, only a few of the more knowledgeable took measures such as the planting of clover to rejuvenate the depleted soil. The ground was tilled by the farmer himself walking behind a horse- or ox-drawn plow, an activity that only experience can prepare one to appreciate.

To supplement the produce of the farm, there were honey

and the native grapes, as well as a variety of wild fruits and berries—apples, cherries, plums, blackberries, strawberries, and raspberries, mulberries, currants, cranberries, and gooseberries. In his idle moments before and after the evening meal, the farmer worked at his woodpile, cutting and stacking logs of fireplace length. The boys of the family saw that the woodbox near the stove and hearth was well stocked; their sisters were often responsible for proper tending of the ovens for baking bread. There was much truth in the saying that wood was a fuel that heated you thrice: first, in the felling of the tree, again when the logs were chopped for the fireplace, and finally as a blaze on the hearth.

On the Sabbath many people were to be found in church, often twice. Among the denominations in New England at the beginning of the nineteenth century were the Congregationalists, Presbyterians, Baptists, Methodists, Episcopalians, Unitarians, Universalists, Roman Catholics, Friends, Shakers, Jews, and many others, including the Moravians, Antinomians, and Sandemanians. In Massachusetts and Connecticut, laws forbade travel on the Sabbath, and were regarded by some as an infringement on personal freedom. Funerals and marriages were important social as well as religious events. Marriages provided the occasion for welcome festivity, with relatives and neighbors invited to a dinner given by the parents of the bride; often the ceremony was conducted in the evening with cake, wine, and dancing for the families and guests. The tolling of the parish bell announced the beginning of the funeral service, and the clergyman offered a prayer at the home of the deceased before the body was carried by hearse or on the shoulders of neighbors to the graveside.

The duties of the clergyman extended far beyond the church. In addition to his two sermons on Sunday, each of which might last 40 minutes or longer, he catechized the young of his flock, visited the sick, received visiting dignitaries, and, as a leading citizen in his community, was obliged to entertain frequently, to attend a wide variety of meetings within his district, and to deliver a number of public and private lectures. In many ways his life was not an easy one. The church in which he preached was often cold, so cold that the parishioners brought their own foot stoves filled with hot coals to warm their toes during the long services. When the length of the services required an intermission, pastor, worshippers, and deacons would repair to a small building, or "Sabbath Day House," next to the church in which there was a roaring fire. When everyone was thawed out, congregation and clergy would return to the Lord's work in the cold church. In more prosperous communities, the church bell might ring at seven in the morning, at noon, and at curfew, about nine o'clock at night. Its ringing announced fires, wars, the day of the month, births, and deaths; sometimes the inventive bellringer used a simple code to announce the sex and age of the deceased. Some even maintained that the practiced ear could detect the direction of the wind and the barometric pressure, and even predict the next day's weather—all from the pealing of the church bell.

One of the most momentous changes to occur in life in New England came with the rise of Unitarianism, Universalism, and other religious splinter groups in the early nineteenth century. The appointment of Henry Ware in 1805 as the Hollis Professor of divinity at Harvard College is regarded by some as the real beginning of fundamental change in religious attitude in New England, although the Unitarian Society had been established in Philadelphia in 1796 by the British scientist, Joseph Priestley. Disputes went on for years between the Unitarians and the more Calvinist-minded of their Congregational brethren. In time the traditionalists grew so dismayed at Harvard College, that former stronghold of Congregationalism, that they founded a new theological school at Andover, Massachusetts to insure a proper setting for the preparation of their clergy. The Unitarians, on their part, were blessed with some of the most persuasive speakers and writers ever to quote the Scriptures; Joseph Buckminster and William Ellery Channing spoke with eloquence for Unitarians, while Hosea Ballou occupied the pulpit of the Second Universalist Church in Boston for 35 years. Other denominations beside the Congregationalists were losing members to the new sects; Alexander Campbell broke with the Presbyterians and later the Baptists to found the Disciples of Christ.

These men and others had begun to see in man virtues denied by the older denominations; moreover, man seemed capable of self-improvement if only he were given a chance. Instead of the austerity and rigid scrupulousness of Calvinism, the Unitarians stressed the amiable and hopeful, and rejected the idea of predestination and the ultimate depravity of man. Salvation was to be achieved through individual integrity, charity toward all, and the love of God. What was to be pursued with fervor was the brotherhood of man and the transformation of life on earth so that the Kingdom of God might be realized by those yet living.

Somehow, man seems to weary after a time of both the "true believer" and the reformer; certainly few religions before or since have placed such a heavy burden for piety and right behavior on the faithful as did that of the Calvinists. But the Revolutions, both American and French, helped to unleash new ideas in the land, ideas that weakened the hold of the strictest of the Congregational clergy and elders. Then, too, the clergy themselves seem in some places to have been almost relieved at the loss of some responsibility for disciplining their flocks. Nevertheless, in many country parishes the autocratic tendencies of the clergy were as strong as ever and the close ties between church, the courts, and other centers of community power were maintained with assiduity. Pulpits thundered against the dangers of Thomas Jefferson and his followers; all Jacobin tendencies were to be destroyed root and branch. Things democratic were equated with all that was evil, and the horrors of the French Revolution were cited as prime examples of what happened when democracy was unleashed on a law-abiding citizenry. The prominent Federalist, Fisher Ames, for example, feared that the election of Thomas

Jefferson meant the end of everything he held sacred; a few even toyed with the idea of separation from the Union.

Public schooling developed in New England as it did nowhere else in the new republic. No higher tribute could be paid to the schools of Massachusetts than these words by Thomas Jefferson in a letter to J. C. Cabell.

Yet it is unquestionable that [Massachusetts] has more influence in our confederacy than any other State in it. Whence this ascendancy? From her attention to education, unquestionably. There can be no stronger proof that knowledge is power, and that ignorance is weakness.

How is one to account for this interest in schooling in New England? The presence of small towns in which it was economically feasible to hire a schoolmaster and to build a school was no doubt a factor. There was also a tradition among the people that learning was to be valued, especially when it could cast light on the mysteries of religion. Furthermore, there was a good deal of social cohesiveness in the North, partly as a result of common language, heritage, dangers, and even religious background, although the constant religious squabbles and schisms make one question the claims to common ground in this area. Perhaps part of the answer springs from the nature of Puritanism itself and the tradition of uncovering truth and avoiding error through assiduous study of the Bible. Deep in the Puritan tradition (popular notions about the excesses of Puritanism notwithstanding) there was a fear of error that compelled the Puritan to listen to an argument, and at its conclusion to attempt to correct the error either in his opponent's thinking or his own, wherever that error manifested itself. Because error was more likely to spring from ignorance, knowledge was to be preferred. To the twentieth-century mind there is a curious obtuseness to this argument, but a moment's reflection will remind us that keeping people in a state of ignorance is still seen as necessary to the maintenance of good order among the masses, or so it seems to some. One of the notable differences between the United States and Europe in the early nineteenth century was that Americans took pride in the fact that they were not peasants, but often landowners; and although they were not learned, neither were they ignorant. No one in America, Timothy Dwight insisted, began with the expectation of remaining a laborer all his life. Instead of fearing that persons of humble origins who acquired a little knowledge and the skill with which to learn would be "apt to rise above their proper station and business," most Americans hoped to be able to better their positions. In New England, as elsewhere, there were those who believed that a little schooling was a good thing for everyone.

The Middle States

Philadelphia in 1800 enjoyed a reputation as the intellectual capital of the nation, and until July of that year, it was the seat of government and the home of the Bank of the United States. The city had a dependable water supply, the best-paved streets in the country, and the best lighting and sanitation systems in the country. There was a turnpike to Lancaster, as well as good roads, canals, and bridges. Washington, D.C., on the other hand, was looked on as a most unhealthy place at the beginning of the nineteenth century; there were a few brick rooming houses, but the White House and the Capitol building were only half finished.

In Pennsylvania, at least 20 different religious denominations were active, the Quakers most prominent among them. In the absence of New England's rigid church oligarchy, or a planter aristocracy, as in Virginia and South Carolina, or the domination of a few wealthy families, as in New York, a relatively tolerant climate prevailed in both religious and political matters. As a result, settlers were attracted from many nations, and the countryside was soon dotted with small farms harboring citizens in search of religious truth and a comfortable living. Among the many nationalities to settle in Pennsylvania were the industrious Germans, who were generally regarded as unusually skillful farmers. Their handsome barns with stone walls, artistic weather vanes, and colorful hex symbols attested to both their skill and pride as workmen. The hex symbols were also found on the quilts sewn by the German women; they were not intended as deterrents to unfriendly spirits, but instead, expressed the same pride of achievement as that of their husbands. It should come as no surprise, therefore, that the Germans were not enthusiastic about schools in which German was not to be the dominant language of instruction.

New York City was home to peoples of many countries; among its 100,000 citizens in 1800 were immigrants from Scotland, Germany, France, Holland, Sweden, Spain, the West Indies, and many other nations. A visitor to the city in the early nineteenth century reported the presence of 55 churches, including 12 Episcopal, 7 Dutch, 7 Presbyterian, 8 Baptist, 7 Methodist, and several of the Scotch-Reform, Quaker, German Lutheran, German Calvinist, Moravian, Universalist, and Roman Catholic persuasions, and a Jewish synagogue. There were the usual public buildings—a city hall, prison. hospital, alms houses for the poor, an orphan asylum, a public library, customs house, and national and state arsenals; two theaters, Columbia College, banks, insurance companies, hotels, coffeehouses, markets, a chamber of commerce, and the halls of the various social organizations, such as the Mechanics Society, the Tammany Society, and the Washington Society. The Tammany Society, an observer remarked, was established to afford relief to persons in distress, but "its principal business is ... believed to be that of influencing elections." Although the Washington Society existed for "benevolent purposes," it, too, was substantially engaged in political activities. A Humane Society in the city attempted to assist debtors, and other groups were formed to aid impoverished immigrants from Germany, Scotland, Ireland, and elsewhere. Columbia College was in operation under the guidance of a president, a provost, and four professors who taught moral philosophy, literature, mathematics, natural philosophy, logic, rhetoric, and belles lettres.

Early nineteenth-century New Yorkers of means attended the theater, assemblies, concerts, and balls; they especially enjoyed horse racing, a popular sport throughout the nation, whether it was of the saddleback variety or harness racing, with the horse pulling a four-wheeled sulky.

Most of the children whose parents had the wherewithal could find a school to attend for a few years; although a common school "system" of sorts existed, the money set aside for the schooling of the poor was insufficient. Consequently, many children were obliged to depend on "apprenticeship, the mercy of God, or charity" for even a modicum of schooling. Despite unregulated schooling practices it is estimated by Carl Kaestle "that over 50 percent of the city's school-age children attended school annually in the 1790's. . . ."

In western New York, away from the Hudson River with its large estates owned by descendants of the early Dutch settlers, the population was dispersed, and it was difficult to find large enough concentrations of people to support a church and retain a well-educated minister. To overcome this lack of spiritual guidance, the missionary societies of New England and New York City sent out clergymen from time to time to preach, administer the sacraments, and distribute Bibles and tracts. In Albany, the second city of the state, the importance of the Dutch influence along the Hudson was attested to by the architecture, the family names, the churches, and many other reminders. Besides the usual public and privately owned buildings, Albany boasted a number of plants processing barley, peas, mustard, and snuff. In these plants boys worked alongside men and were provided with the educational experiences, both good and bad, that such relationships have always engendered.

The South

The child growing to maturity in the South in the early national period spent a relatively short part of his life in school, less, perhaps, than his counterpart in New England. In the South the soil was fertile and the climate well suited to the growing of valuable export crops that could be transported on navigable rivers on the way to market. The plantation dominated the life of tidewater Virginia; agriculture and the rural outlook determined the events and the character of the people. Tobacco was a major export for most of the early national period, but with the invention of the cotton gin, cotton became the most important export crop, especially after the War of 1812. In addition to the large plantations there were small inland farms and towns, of which only Charleston was of a size to rival the cities of Boston, Philadelphia, and New York. In 1800, Virginia had the largest population of any state in the Union, and North Carolina had more inhabitants than Massachusetts. However, the westward migration was heavy in the early nineteenth century, and by 1830 there were almost as many people in Ohio as in Virginia. There were Irishmen and Scots-Irishmen in Virginia and the Carolinas; French Huguenots in South Carolina, and a mixture of other nationalities spread throughout the South, but for the most part, the Southerners of the time were English in descent.

Altogether 2½ million people lived in the South by 1800; however, almost 1 million were blacks, and of this number only about 50,000 were freemen. The first slaves arrived in the United States in 1619, even before the Pilgrims. Purchased in Africa, the West Indies, and elsewhere—often from other black men—the slaves were brought to the American continent in the holds of ships captained by Englishmen, Dutchmen, Americans, and others, to be sold at public auction. Broadsides offered human beings for sale in words similar to the following:

To be sold, on Thursday the third Day of August next, a cargo of ninety-four prime, healthy Negroes, consisting of thirty-nine Men, Fifteen Boys, Twenty-four Women, and Sixteen Girls. Just arrived, in the Brigantine, Dembia, Francis Bore, Master, from Sierra-Leon, by David & John Deas.

The distance between social groups was probably greater in the South than in other parts of the country. The plantation owner and his family isolated themselves from the tradesmen of the small towns, and the small farmer of the Piedmont or Georgia probably had more in common with his counterpart in the West than he did with the plantation owner of his own region. Between the plantation owner and his slaves, a network of complex relationships bridged a yawning social chasm. Among the slaves themselves was a distinction based on the work and the disposition of the master. The field slave toiled day in and day out in the fields planted to cotton, tobacco, rice, sugar, hemp, or other crops; often his wife and family worked beside him. The skilled artisan, on the other hand, lived on or near the plantation house or in a small town where he enjoyed more personal autonomy, and sometimes was able to associate with free Negroes, or even to buy his freedom and that of his family, a practice that was common in South America, but less so in North America. A few of the skills possessed by slaves were carpentry, woodworking and cabinetmaking, blacksmithing, leatherworking, weaving, distilling, and wheelwrighting.

Enjoying a still better life than either the field hand or the artisan was the "driver" who served as the overseer's assistant. Exempt from field work himself, he was given better fare and privileges denied other workers. In return it was his responsibility to see that the work was done, that punishment was administered, and that the task of the overseer went smoothly.

Of the enslaved blacks, however, the highest on the social scale were the household domestics—the maidservants, butler, coachman, nurses, and cooks. Sometimes these slaves were given quarters in a wing of the plantation, and under an unusually benevolent master, they might almost come to be regarded as members of the family—almost, but never quite. The plantation owner who employed a tutor for his own children might permit, if kindly disposed, the children of the domestics and other slaves to receive a little instruction by sitting at the back of the schoolroom to listen to the recitations and lessons of the white pupils. One of the most tragic facts of American history is that later it actually became illegal in many places in the South to give instruction to the children of slaves; these laws were passed in the old traditional view that learning was power, and power in the hands of slaves was dangerous.

Nor was the fear of slave revolts entirely imaginary. A slave named Gabriel attempted a revolt in 1800 and was hanged, along with 30 followers; Nat Turner led a revolt in 1831 that resulted in his death and the deaths of his black followers and a number of whites, as well. Although these poorly organized and executed slave revolts had little chance for success, the fear of a large-scale uprising haunted the dreams of Southerners for generations.

The more successful tactics of resistance open to the slave were much the same as those used by the laborers in the nineteenth and twentieth centuries who were intent on establishing unions—the slowdown and covert destruction of property by fire and sabotage. And, of course, it was sometimes possible for the slave to run away to an uncertain future in the North or in Canada, but this usually meant leaving his family and friends behind forever. If he were caught he might be lashed— often by a public flogger—and possibly branded; or what was worse, he might be dubbed as incorrigible and sold to a master more cruel than the one from whom he had run. Needless to say, none of the prospects before him seemed particularly bright.

During the American Revolution, black men, both free and slave, served on both sides, but with few exceptions, in the lowest ranks. Almost every town in the state of Connecticut sent one or more blacks to the war, and many other towns in New England and the Middle States did the same. Of all the blacks who took part in the American Revolution, the most famous was Crispus Attucks, a runaway slave who was killed in the "Boston Massacre" of 1770. Blacks were to be found serving in many regiments and made up a sizable proportion of a few infantry units such as the First Rhode Island. It was common to find one or more blacks serving on privateers. One such sailor was James Forten, who served aboard a privateer commissioned by the state of Pennsylvania. After the war, Forten returned to Philadelphia, acquired a fortune, and became an ardent abolitionist.

In the South, blacks were put to work building bridges and fortifications, carrying supplies, and performing other tasks that would free a white for active soldiering. During the Revolution the British employed the same strategy that prompted Lincoln's Emancipation Proclamation 90 years later, and offered runaway slaves their freedom as well as the opportunity to practice any trade they possessed if they would desert to the British lines. With this inducement, they attracted several thousand, and when the redcoats left the country after the defeat at Yorktown, many blacks went with them, some as slaves of British soldiers and other as free men.

A few abolitionist societies had begun during the Revolutionary War, among them the "Pennsylvania Society for Promoting the Abolition of Slavery, the Relief of Free Negroes unlawfully held in Bondage and Improving the Condition of the African Race." The postwar period saw the establishment of abolitionist societies in such states as Delaware, Maryland, Virginia, New Jersey, Connecticut, Kentucky, and Rhode Island. John Jay served as first president of the "Society for the Promoting of the Manumission of Slaves" in New York; Benjamin Franklin had the same role in Pennsylvania, with Benjamin Rush as his successor. A convention of abolitionist societies was held in Philadelphia in 1794, under the auspices of the Pennsylvania and New York bodies.

In the early nineteenth century, these abolition groups tended to become moribund; in time they were replaced—in the 1830s and 1840s—by a much more militant antislavery movement, the objective of which was not only the abolition of slavery in the United States, but also the "intellectual, moral, and religious improvement" of the racial minorities and the eradication of public prejudice against all such persons.

Nevertheless, the early abolitionist societies served a useful function in their attempts to protect runaway slaves, to find jobs for them, and, perhaps most important, to keep the runaways from being sold back into slavery. The New York Manumission Society founded the African Free School in 1787; beginning with 40 pupils, the school made an attempt to provide the children of former slaves with the schooling and skills necessary to a new life under freedom.

Various religious groups were opposed to slavery—the Methodists, who were greatly influenced by the preaching of John Wesley, and the Baptists, who licensed black preachers, both slave and free. But it was the Quakers in whom opposition to slavery ran deepest. In response to heightened sentiment among religious bodies, to the appeals to principles that had brought on the Revolution, and to demands for simple human decency, the various states began to pass laws abolishing or restricting slavery. In New Jersey, for example, slavery was to be abolished after 1804, but the steps toward that abolishment were to be gradual. In Virginia and Maryland there was some antislavery sentiment after the Revolution. However, there was little antislavery sentiment in the deep South. Although the Northwest Ordinance of 1787 contained a provision against the spread of slavery to the new territories, the real hopes of the antislavery forces lay with the delegates to the Constitutional Convention of 1787. As we have seen, however, the Convention actually prevented the restriction on the slave trade for 20 years. Those who thought that slavery would die a natural death if given a little time were proved wrong by the growing demand for cotton cloth, the invention of cotton-processing machinery, and the acquisition of Louisiana, Florida, and Texas, which vastly increased the acreage available for cotton cultivation. These changes converted the American South to the world's leading source for cotton. Tragically, then, the institution of slavery received a new burst of life in the early nineteenth century.

In 1808 the importation of slaves was made illegal, but by that time the production of cotton was increasing rapidly, and it took little imagination to see that it would be a most profitable commodity, indeed. So the smuggling of slaves became a profitable venture. Furthermore, while the law slowed the importation of slaves from Africa, the demand was so great that smuggling became highly profitable and slaves were brought to the cotton-growing regions from other places within the United States. New Orleans became one of the centers of the interstate slave trade with individuals and even whole families put on the block, the latter groups to be sold intact or broken up at the pleasure of the buyer.

Conditions had been bad, but they were to grow worse after 1822 with the passage of the laws such as those prohibiting the education of slaves. These so-called "slave codes" not only restricted the slaves, but they also made life harder for the 180,000 freemen of a black population of over 2 million living in the South by 1830. These "free" blacks could own property and make contracts, but they were seldom allowed to hold any public office or to vote; they were often subject to travel restrictions and could not own firearms.

chapter three
the frontier

Visitors to the United States at the beginning of the nineteenth century found a land stretching 1000 miles along the Atlantic Ocean with no sizable cities of 100,000 or more inhabitants. Travel westward was difficult, although a wagon road ran through the Cumberland Gap; further north were Braddock's and Forbes' Roads, both of which had been used in pre-Revolutionary War times for travel by the military. By 1818 the National (or Cumberland) Road, following Braddock's Road for a portion of its route, reached all the way from Cumberland, Maryland to Wheeling, West Virginia. Travel from Philadelphia to Pittsburgh was by way of the Kittanning Path. As early as 1800 over half a million people had used these and other routes to seek adventure and wealth in the fertile valleys of Ohio, Kentucky, and Tennessee. When the trails petered out at the water's edge, the settlers would often build a raft and float down the Ohio River until they came to land they could buy at auction, sometimes for as little as $1 an acre. This westward rush grew in intensity with the end of the War of 1812, with the appearance of steamboats on the Ohio in 1818, and with the completion of the Erie Canal in 1825; by the 1830s the frontier had been pushed as far west as Iowa, Missouri, and Arkansas. Nevertheless, the pioneers were still only about one third of the way across the continent, and some of the most difficult terrain still lay ahead.

The motives for moving west were as various as the men and women who made the trek. Some writers have described the settlers who made up the cutting edge of frontier society as restless men with little patience for the day-to-day drudgery of farming, men who preferred instead to erect a lean-to as a temporary shelter and then sell their land to the first new-comer who had the wherewithal to buy. Unquestionably there were malcontents in the ranks of those who moved west, men who would always choose unknown dangers and rumored opportunities over the tangible problems of the workaday world. Sometimes it is more painful to remain than to move on; however, those who stayed on their land were perhaps not displeased to see the malcontents leave. But there were others who moved west. Settlers with growing families sought vaster and richer lands than they could find in New England or in Pennsylvania. Immigrants believed the west promised more opportunity than did the more settled east, and former neighbors and friends of earlier pioneers were persuaded to follow in the footsteps of their friends, lured by tales of inexpensive land and flowing riches.

One of the first tasks the settler faced when he reached his new acres was the building of a lean-to, as close to water as possible, to shelter his family, his livestock, and his tools. Next, he cut down the surrounding trees to clear the land for cultivation, or he "girdled" them, slashing the bark all around the trunk to prevent nourishment from reaching the top. In time the trees would die, and later they would be cut and burned, or used as firewood or in building. With the trees dead, the settler could cultivate the land with a harrow or "drag," a frame formed like the letter "A" with iron spikes driven through it. A plow with a deeper bite than the harrow would do a better job of turning up the ground, but it would also catch the roots of dead trees and break both itself and the harness. Dragged over the ground several times this "A" frame dug the earth in preparation for seed corn, wheat, or some other crop. As the seedlings sprouted there were no leaves in the girdled trees to prevent rain and sunlight from nourishing the crops. After harvest in the autumn the dead trees were cut and burned; sometimes the ash was used to make soap, and the rest was scattered over the fields as fertilizer.

With his family and animals protected by a rough log shelter, and a crop growing under newly tilled fields, the settler turned his attention to the task of securing more comfortable living quarters. In frontier America this usually meant a log house, a barn, and outbuildings such as sheds. Each log for this construction was stripped of bark and hewn on two opposite sides. Each end of the hewn sides was cut to half-thickness to form a joint with the log laid at right angles to it. Wooden pins were used when necessary to secure beams, and cracks were sealed with whatever mortar was at hand. Sometimes the roof was covered with shake shingles carefully split from straight grained wood; there was a fireplace made of stone, and in some cabins there was a window that, if made of precious glass, was easily removed should the settler sell his land and buildings and go in search of a new home. A loft above the regular quarters provided sleeping space for the children; the floor was dirt or rough planking sprinkled with sand. The same techniques used in the construction of the house were employed in erecting a permanent barn. The settler fortunate enough to have nearby kin or congenial neighbors might be the host at a "barn raising," a function that combined work and play for both the men and boys who erected the building, and for the women and girls who prepared food and drink for the workers and exchanged the gossip of the day. Often prayers accompanied such communal efforts as did such activities as horse racing, games, and log-adzing contests. Rustic humor in the United States has long taken note of the fact that the barn the farmer built for his animals was sometimes more commodious than the house that sheltered his family. Obviously the joke was enjoyed more by the farmer than by his wife and children.

There were satisfactions in being a farmer on the western frontier. In time the crops ripened and were harvested; animals grew fat and were slaughtered; the family grew in size and productivity; buildings acquired an inside coat of whitewash, and more land was added to the family holdings. But the farmer often paid a heavy price for his gains: his isolation, with its concomitant loneliness, resulted sometimes in melancholia for his wife, in the constant dread of Indian attack, a threat that was by turns real and imaginary, in the fear of disease, toothache, and crippling injury with medical and dental care beyond reach, and in too infrequent visits by a circuit-riding clergyman who attended to questions of the soul. Those who lived in or close to settlements were only slightly more fortunate, since everywhere throughout the west lurked the danger of sudden and violent extinction at the hands of a variety of enemies. Fortunately, when crops failed, there was usually sufficient game to meet the needs of the family if the hunting and fishing skills of father and son were keen.

And there were advantages to being a frontier settler. In a land in which hard work was a necessity, and, therefore, a virtue, the fruits of one's labors could be enjoyed with special relish. Sleep is truly refreshing when it follows a hard day of solid accomplishment in the field; food, even the simplest fare, tastes better when the appetite is sharpened by work and weather; a visit from friends bearing all the news becomes more meaningful when it enlivens one of a series of endless solitary days. The children watched all this, and they worked hard and they learned.

On the frontier, matters of life and death took precedence over schemes for formal schooling; indeed, it was unclear what benefits schooling might afford aside from the obvious advantages to be had from reading, writing, and reckoning. The views of men such as Benjamin Rush, Thomas Jefferson, and Noah Webster who hoped that formal schooling might be a means of unifying the country seemed mere abstractions to the frontiersman. To Europeans a sense of unity was to be found in the institution of the monarchy, in a common language and heritage, in the church, or even in the military. Many Americans, on the other hand, came to the new land seeking to escape the repressions of a monarchical government or a state church; after the Revolution, many became justifiably suspicious of a well-organized military. To the Westerners, a few lessons taught in a schoolroom were scarcely the stuff out of which national unity might be forged; indeed, the very question of nationhood seemed unimportant or remote when local problems were so absorbing. To the extent that schooling could contribute to the solution of these problems, it was admitted to be a useful thing. Advanced schooling, on the other hand, was something to be sought only as a refinement by clergymen, schoolmasters, and other professionals with a scholarly turn of mind; it was, in short, not absolutely necessary to life on the frontier, and, consequently, was of a second order of priority.

A primary force impelling the American people westward in the early national period was, of course, the prospect of greater opportunity in a new society that still placed relatively few restrictions on the individual. The fact that some of the less scrupulous would abuse this freedom to exploit their fellows and despoil the land could not tarnish the appeal to the imagination of an ever-expanding frontier.

Forgotten or ignored by some earlier history books was the havoc wreaked by the European when his culture—dynamic, acquisitive, dogmatic, proud, superstitious, intolerant, well-organized, and energetic—encountered the society of the Indian—familial and tribal in pattern, proud, individualistic, warlike, eloquent, superstitious, and artistic. The Indian was given an intolerable choice. He could join the more powerful invader and abandon a life of hunting, fishing, and light agriculture for heavy agriculture and shop skills and watching as tribal territory became the white man's private property, or he could move on. Gradually the Indian had to yield to the white man's pressure; often he was forcibly removed from his ancestral home.

At the time of their first encounter with European man, there were 1 million Indians in North America, most of them living along the Atlantic and Pacific Coastal Plains and in what is now the Gulf states. The basic political and social unit was the family existing within the tribe; each tribe was self-contained and independent, although from time to time confederacies or leagues were formed for protection against other such groups or the Europeans. There may have been as many as 2000 North American tribes speaking in as many as 51 distinct language families as well as many more dialects.

To the Indian, land was as free as the wind and the water; the idea that it could be bought and sold was difficult to comprehend. And even if the land were sold to the white man for agriculture, surely this did not prevent Indians from hunting deer and elk on that land, or from catching the fish in its streams. Furthermore, since the land, the clouds, the air, and the sea were given by the Great Spirit to all, no single person or tribe could claim exclusive right to them forever. Dozens of treaties were concluded with the Indians in the early national period in which huge sections of land—sometimes whole states —were ceded to the federal government, or more rarely to private companies, often in return for goods or money, or promises. A few of these treaties were Hopewell, 1785; New York City, 1790; Holston River, 1795; Treaty of Tellico, 1798; Buffalo Creek, 1802; Vincennes, 1803; Fort Clark, 1808; St. Louis, 1816; Old Town, 1818; and Saginaw, 1819. Later many Indians living in the East, the South, and the Ohio territory were rounded up and moved West of the Mississippi River, many of them to the Indian Territory of Oklahoma, where untold numbers succumbed to disease, exposure, and despair. There, too, they came in contact with the fierce, nomadic Plains Indians, who would meet the same fate later in the nineteenth century.

From a rich storehouse of Indian mythology, the young

learned the stories of the "Woman Who Married a Star," "The Lost Children," "The Twin Brothers," and the "Origin of the Pleiades." They were also taught the skills needed in hunting and planting, tanning and leatherworking, the fashioning of stone weapons and tools, the traditional tribal dances, and the values shared by the community.

Tribal affairs were conducted by adult males of the tribe who gathered around a council fire to have forceful and eloquent speakers reply to the questions at issue put before them by the chief or his designate. At the close of discussion someone with special skill would summarize what had been said, and then the prevailing opinion would be determined. If the question was a weighty one, these councils might last a week or longer. Various missionary societies, both American and European, attempted to Christianize the Indians, but met with indifferent success. Several American colleges, including William and Mary and Dartmouth, began with plans to educate Indian boys in the skills of reading, writing, arithmetic, and the tenets of Christianity. A few Indians were converted, and a handful even became clergymen who preached in the United States and sometimes returned as missionaries to their own people. Most Indians, however, resisted attempts to make them embrace Christianity and other aspects of European culture. On the other hand, the white man's firearms, tools, blankets, food, and other commodities were welcome, but the Indian would discover, to his sorrow, the price ultimately exacted for these goods.

Efforts of the missionaries were usually at least two pronged; they sought both to Christianize and to "civilize" the Indian. To civilize often meant to convert the Indian to all the ways of the white man, including the substitution of English for their native tongue. Efforts to conduct instruction in English often met with little success, but when the missionaries took the trouble to learn the Indian's speech and to instruct in that language, his efforts were more effective. The government was so intent on the enculturation of the Indian that treaties often contained provision for Christianization and education or both, with the government footing the bill for both clergymen and schoolmasters, as well as persons "to teach [the Indians] to make fences, cultivate the earth, and such of the domestic arts as are adapted to their situation...." Sometimes, too, the federal authorities gave funds to private persons and associations as a supplement to their efforts at schooling the Indians. And the Indians themselves set aside funds, when they could spare them, for the instruction of the young. Of course, the number of Indian students in schools was infinitesimal compared to the potential school-aged group. One estimate made about 1829 was that perhaps 1300 Indian youths were "enjoying the benefits of education."

The way in which some Indians must have regarded these "benefits" is conveyed by this polite rejection of an early offer of schooling attributed to a tribal spokesman and reprinted in a book by Samuel G. Drake, published in 1845.

We know that you highly esteem the kind of learning taught in those colleges, and that the maintenance of our young men, while with you, would be very expensive to you. We are convinced, therefore, that you mean to do us good by your proposal.... We have had some experience of it: several of our young people were formerly brought up at the colleges of the northern provinces; they were instructed in all your sciences; but when they came back to us, they were bad runners; ignorant of every means of living in the woods; unable to bear either cold or hunger; knew neither how to build a cabin, take a deer, or kill an enemy; spoke our language imperfectly; were therefore neither fit for hunters, warriors, or counsellors; they were totally good for nothing.... If the gentlemen of Virginia will send us a dozen of their sons, we will take great care of their education, instruct them in all we know, and make men of them.

In combination with such sturdy virtues as frugality, a capacity for hard work, and trust in the future, the opportunity that awaited the white settler, however, would prove to be no myth. This visible affirmation of man's desire to improve his lot and his ability to do so under conditions of freedom and equality had a powerful impact on the thought and ideas of a society sobered by the upheavals of the American and French Revolutions. The heightened human expectations were reflected in the new ideas promulgated in the eighteenth and nineteenth centuries; ideas that strengthened the concept of man as a creature with some control over his own destiny, with responsibility to improve the human condition instead of bowing to a divine will that decreed for some a life of pain and degradation and suffering. There were renewed arguments, too, for a reinterpretation of the role of government in the lives of the citizens, of government as the servant of the people, not their master, as the dispenser of justice, not favors. And there was a new appreciation of man—European man, at any rate—as a creature of intellect, intuition, and a capacity for goodness as well as evil. Very gradually, the argument that declared every man to be the political equal of any other was extended to imply social equality as well.

Many Americans of the time were familiar with theories of freedom and government propounded by writers such as Locke and Montesquieu, as well as by the Greek philosophers and Roman essayists. In addition, they were aware of the principles behind the rationalism of Voltaire and the new knowledge and techniques destined to generate still more knowledge that were the contributions of Descartes, Newton, Bacon, Cavendish, Galvani, Lavoisier, Harvey, Boyle, and others. Of course, the scientific studies of these men were to revolutionize human life; perhaps equally significant, they would remind man of the great power inherent in his capacity to think, to experiment, and to create. Separately, each of these ideas on political and social equality and the discoveries in the nature of man's environment was extremely potent; in combination they were to be irresistible and were to remake the world.

In time, ideas such as the perfectability of man, of his political and social equality before the law, and of government as an instrument of man's progress rather than of his enslavement were all to be tested in the crucible of human experience. So, too, the value of the power of reason and of scientific endeavor would one day be judged by the degree to which they contributed to the welfare of the individual man, and the test is still underway. As congenial as these principles of justice and opportunity were to the American mind, they were sometimes honored more in theory than in practice. It seems unlikely, for example, that men who duped the Indian and forced him from his ancestral lands wasted much time in pondering why one man's opportunity should be another's disaster; and when the profits in cotton growing were great enough to tempt a saint, there were men who found it expedient to insist that the concept of the equality of man was limited, of course, to free men.

One must recognize in this connection that the Founding Fathers were not only familiar with contemporary European thought, but also with the history, literature, and customs of ancient Greece and Rome. It has been suggested, in fact, that with their knowledge of and their natural affinity for the classical mode, Thomas Jefferson, Alexander Hamilton, and James Madison would have been quite comfortable in togas. Indeed, the study of classical language and literature was a staple of the early colleges in the United States. But whatever advantages the knowledge of those older civilizations may have afforded the fathers of the American republic—and they were undeniably great—they could not have failed to confront the fact that both those ancient societies were based on human slavery. Consequently, there were undoubtedly men in important positions who assumed that slavery was inevitable, even in a representative democracy. Even those who regarded slavery as an evil to be abolished as soon as possible were not sanguine in their hopes for a move toward emancipation. Surely Thomas Jefferson knew the true horror of slavery when he wrote: "I tremble for my country when I reflect that God is just, that his justice cannot sleep forever. Commerce between master and slave is despotism. Nothing is more certainly written in the book of fate than that these people are to be free." It was the failure to deal outright with the institution of slavery that has brought shame, degradation, and death to generations of Americans, white as well as black.

chapter four
the arts and crafts

If a nation expects to be ignorant and free, in a state of civilization, it expects what never was and never will be. Letter from Thomas Jefferson to Colonel Charles Yancey, January 6, 1816.

$\mathfrak{t}$he process of education in any society depends not just on schoolmaster and parent for its content and the method of its transmission, but on the cumulative efforts of the thinker and doer in every field of human endeavor: the philosopher, the artist, the mathematician, the architect, the scientist, the politician, the mechanic, the engineer, and the farmer.

The United States in the early national period produced little to compare with the European contributions in scholarly learning, the arts, sciences, and literature. To the chagrin of Americans such as Noah Webster and Benjamin Rush and later, Ralph Waldo Emerson, Americans were still dependent on European culture. That there were exceptions to this will be seen later; for the most part, however, American education was based on the higher learning, the art, and the philosophy of post--Renaissance Europe—on the work of Michelangelo and Da Vinci, Locke, Bacon, Newton, Hume, and Descartes, Rousseau, Montaigne, and Condorcet, Berkeley, Priestley, Samuel Johnson, and Edmund Burke; on the literary genius of Shakespeare and Goethe, Wordsworth, Lamb, Coleridge, Scott, Keats, and Shelley. It was to the centers of European learning—London, Rome, Paris, Berlin, and Edinburgh—that Americans traveled for culture, inspiration, and instruction.

To be sure, there were Americans of great skill and learning. Benjamin Franklin and Thomas Jefferson were unusually gifted men by any standard, and their contributions to invention, science, architecture, political philosophy, and letters would be the envy of any people on earth; the American mathematician and amateur astronomer, Nathaniel Bowditch, wrote *The New American Practical Navigator*, which went through 60 printings and was adopted by the navies of both England and France.

Besides men like Franklin, Jefferson, and Bowditch, who enjoyed international reputations for their work, there were men and women at work within the United States who earned little fame beyond their homeland, and who certainly would not rank among the most influential and inspired of geniuses when compared with the European luminaries. Nonetheless, they were the harbingers of a new day of scientific, technological, literary, and artistic achievement that would in time be admired throughout the world. Jedidiah Morse, father of the painter and inventor Samuel F. B. Morse, was such a man. A Congregational minister, he wrote books on geography that served as texts in American schools for many years. At Princeton, Union College, the University of Pennsylvania, Miami of Ohio, Rensselaer Polytechnic Institute, and other institutions, a few men were beginning to offer special courses for students interested in the study of science. At the Military Academy at West Point, applied science was of prime importance for the future officers and engineers of the Republic. At the Albany Academy and later at Princeton, Joseph Henry, who became first head of the Smithsonian Institution in 1846, conducted experiments in electromagnetism that were later to make him famous.

If one were looking for the signs of future development in the United States, however, it would be profitable to examine the work of the inventors, both American and European, whose machines, when equipped with steam power, would revolutionize the country and even change the face of the earth. Eli Whitney's cotton gin both revolutionized the making of cotton cloth and stiffened the cruel hand of slavery; perhaps this invention and others of the same era were more important than the War of 1812 in determining the future course of the United States. The history books devote much attention to the battles of that war; battles are, after all, more exciting than most inventions. The steamboats launched by John Fitch at Philadelphia and Robert Fulton at New York revolutionized transport. Production of nails by machine had a heavy impact on home construction; and the reaper, one of the first of which was built by Cyrus H. McCormick and tested near Steele's Tavern, Virginia, in July 1831, changed forever the method by which crops were harvested.

In 1803 a visitor to a firearms factory in New Haven, Connecticut, built by Eli Whitney, wrote:

In this manufactory muskets are made in a manner, which I believe to be singular. In forming the various parts of this instrument, machinery moved by water, and remarkably adapted in every instance to the purpose in view, is employed for hammering, cutting, turning, perforating, grinding, polishing, etc. etc.

The proportion and relative position of the several parts of the locks are so exactly alike, and the screws, springs, and other limbs, are made so similar, that they may be transferred from one lock and adjusted to another without any material alteration. This desirable object Mr. Whitney has accomplished by an apparatus, which is simple, peculiar, and eminently ingenious. By an application of the same principles a much greater uniformity has also been given to every part of the muskets made in this manufactory, than can be found in those, which are fabricated at any other. The advantages, which in actual service result from this uniformity, are too obvious to need an explanation.

True indeed. These inventions and techniques and many others like them were to have a profound influence (both good and bad) on the life of Americans when the industrial revolution came to full flower later in the century. Life became what it had never been before, and, of course, so did the education of the young.

Among poets at work in the early national period were Philip Freneau, who wrote patriotic verse popular in his lifetime, and Joel Barlow, both of whom were friends of Thomas Jefferson. Barlow served as a chaplain in the Revolution and as a foreign consul, and he was the author of an unusually interesting plan for an American national university to be chartered by Congress in Washington, D.C. and devoted to research and publication of scholarly papers. Perhaps his most famous poem, "The Columbiad," is little read today because, like so much written after the Revolution, it rhapsodizes on the American past and the glorious future envisioned for the grand Republic. Barlow was one of the so-called "Hartford Wits," an informal literary society, several of whose members were graduates of Yale College. Among the "Wits," who met from time to time to read their satiric verses dealing with various contemporary questions, were Timothy Dwight, John Trumbull, Lemuel Hopkins, and Richard Alsop.

Some of the many writers of the period are still read today. Washington Irving, for example, published his *The History of New York* in 1809 under the pseudonym, Diedrich Knickerbocker. James Fenimore Cooper, whose Leatherstocking Tales are now chiefly the province of juvenile readers, wrote *The Spy, The Last of the Mohicans, The Pioneers, The Pilot*, and *Precaution*, all before 1830. Charles Brockden Brown, one of the few writers who seems to have made the bulk of his living by his writing, was the author of such books as *Wieland, Ormond*, and *Edgar Huntly*. Hugh H. Brackenridge published in four volumes between 1792 and 1797 *Modern Chivalry*, a novel that was for its time somewhat picaresque. Nor was the feminine viewpoint unrepresented among the ranks of the best-selling authors; indeed, Susanna Rowson wrote several novels, including the durable *Charlotte: A Tale of Truth*, first published in London in 1791 and in Philadelphia a few years later. This book, which appeared under several titles, went through an incredible 160 editions.

Royall Tyler's play, *The Contrast*, produced in 1787 is said to have been one of the first produced in America in which professional actors played the parts.

With the appearance in 1815 of the highly respected *North American Review*, edited by William Tudor, American poets and essayists were provided with another outlet for their literary efforts. Thousands of schoolchildren of this century as well as the last committed to memory lines from "Thanatopsis" and "To a Water Fowl," poems by William Cullen Bryant that first appeared in the *Review*.

Americans seem to have always been inordinately fond of forming organizations for one purpose or another. In 1810 in Boston a number of societies existed to pursue literary and scholarly endeavors, for example, the American Academy of Arts and Sciences, American Antiquarian Society, the Massachusetts Historical Society, the Boston Library Society, and the Boston Athenaeum with its large library. One group, The Anthology Society, was composed of prominent Bostonians such as John Kirkland, Joseph Buckminster, William Emerson, and George Ticknor, who met from time to time to talk over the questions of the day and to discuss the quality of papers that had been submitted for publication in the society's periodical, *The Monthly Anthology and Boston Review*.

To the question of whether all this literary effort constituted significant contribution to the poetry and prose of the world, the answer is equivocal. But it did mark the beginning of what was to become in time a strong literary tradition. It was, understandably, difficult for a professional writer to earn enough to support his family in a country in which few people had the money to buy books in any quantity. Furthermore, only a few Americans, such as Aaron Burr, had the wealth and inclination to serve as patrons of the arts, and few families were sufficiently wealthy to allow a son or daughter to undertake a career of writing without regard to financial return. Then, too, Americans were an active people absorbed in business, trade, and agriculture, with little time for sedentary pursuits. And it must be recalled that in many circles, reading novels was frowned on as a peculiarly European taste and therefore somehow frivolous and corrupt; at best it was something to indulge in only after one had fulfilled one's duty by way of Bible study and devotions. It must not be inferred from this fact that Americans did not read; they did, and they read the work of European novelists and essayists as well as native authors partly because no copyright laws as yet restricted the pirating of European publications. When a publisher has no worries about the royalties to be paid an author, he finds it more profitable to publish the works of foreigners than those of his own countrymen, who are in a position to demand a certain percentage of the profit on each book sold.

By the end of the early national period, Americans were beginning to show greater interest in periodicals such as the *North American Review* and the *American Journal of Science and Arts*. But it was the newspaper that was avidly consumed by the reading public; by 1810 over 300 papers, 30 of them appearing daily and many more appearing biweekly were being published. By 1786 the *Pittsburgh Gazette* was being published by John Scull and Joseph Hall. Soon Kentucky and Tennessee could boast gazettes of their own. New York, Philadelphia, and Charleston had daily newspapers soon after the Revolution. The Philadelphia paper, *Aurora*, was judged by Henry Adams to have been both energetic and slanderous. In time other papers appeared; such as the *National Intelligencer*, the *New York Evening Post*, and the *Morning Chronicle*. These early papers were often the voice of one or another political camp and were for that reason sometimes referred to as "storehouses of political calumny." Few of them retained reporters whose prime responsibility was the objective reporting of facts. Instead, they often reprinted long extracts from English periodicals, offered columns of political opinion, reported ship sailings and arrivals, announced auctions, repeated gossip, and printed advertisements.

Beside the family Bible, which was sometimes donated to the master of the house by one of the several missionary societies busy in the Lord's work, most home bookshelves were graced by an almanac. One of the most famous of these was *Poor Richard's Almanac*, the work of Benjamin Franklin, which was published for a quarter of a century. Another almanac that appeared in rural New England in 1793 under the editorship of Robert B. Thomas is still published today as *The Old Farmer's Almanac*. In addition to weather predictions and suggestions as to the best time to plant varieties of crops, the almanac offered its readers riddles, cures and home remedies, sermons, and all manner of sage advice. And there was doggerel:

> *While the bright sun in centre glows,*
> *The earth in annual motion round it goes;*
> *At the same time on its own axis reels,*
> *And gives us change of seasons as it wheels.*

If American literature was in its infancy, its political writing and essays were unsurpassed in the maturity of their philosophy and the richness of their prose; the headiest examples of this genre are, of course, the Declaration of Independence and the Constitution of the United States, as well as the constitutions of the various states. But there were hundreds of other lesser-known political writings—broadsides, tracts, pamphlets, and essays—that betray a grasp of and a concern for political principles unexcelled anywhere in the world. The taut, persuasive prose of Madison, Hamilton, and Jay in *The Federalist Papers* is as good as anything man has ever produced. And the extensive personal correspondence of Washington, Jefferson,

Hamilton, Rush, Adams, and many others bears the imprint of thoughtful men striving to bring forth a new society without destroying the best of the old.

Music

Aside from the hymns of Lowell Mason and others, there was little American music that could be classed as important. However, musical societies were formed in several cities, including the Musical Fund Society of Philadelphia of 1820, the Boston Handel and Haydn Society, founded in 1815, and the Philharmonic Society of New York in 1842. New Orleans was one of the first American cities to enjoy grand opera, and in 1825 Manuel Garcia brought an opera company to New York City. Francis Hopkinson wrote a few musical compositions, including the cantata, *The Temple of Minerva*, but like many of his contemporaries, he was versatile, and besides being a composer, he was a practicing lawyer, a legislator, the author of a number of political satires, and a designer of seals, coins, and flags. In the early national period no American composer appeared to rival such European luminaries as Gluck, Haydn, Mozart, Beethoven, Weber, Rossini, or Schubert.

Furniture

The early national period saw the heyday of a surprising number of furniture makers and other craftsmen. Sometimes called the Federal Period, the era may have been the most dynamic ever in American furniture making. Furniture was usually produced in the five popular styles of the day: Chippendale, Hepplewhite, Sheraton, Directoire, and Empire. Fine pieces such as a side chair with a delicate lyre between the two back crosspieces were prized by city and country folk alike. Working in mahogany, birch, cherry, and other woods, these American craftsmen created variations on the styles of the day with stunning effect to produce grandfather clocks, bureaus with mirrors attached, candlesticks, and other household pieces eagerly sought today by antique dealers and householders with an eye to beauty in design and workmanship. Philadelphia-style highboys and lowboys, for example, are still highly esteemed and sometimes bring sums at auctions in the tens of thousands of dollars. Working in Philadelphia at about this time were Thomas Affleck, William Savery, and Benjamin Randolph; in the South, Charleston was regarded as the center of cabinet and fine furniture work. In Newport, Rhode Island, were the workshops of the Townsend and Goddard families, famous for three generations for their fine block-front furniture. Salem was known for the work of the Sanderson family with the special carvings of Samuel McIntire and his son. Duncan Phyfe and Charles Honoré Lannuier worked in New York.

Pewter and Glass

Other fine craftsmen were at work, also. From earliest colonial days men were making dishes, bowls, cups, teapots, and other household utensils of pewter, a ware made of tin combined with other metals, usually copper or lead (or both) with bismuth or antimony added. The mixture was then poured into brass molds to be shaped into useful articles. Sometimes, after years of use, pewter utensils were returned to a pewterer to be melted and recast. To be a worker in pewter, a boy served a long apprenticeship; if he worked with his father, he might be fortunate enough to inherit the expensive brass molds and tools with which to start his own workshop. In Connecticut, the Danforth family followed pewtering for generations. In New York, the Bassetts produced tankards that are highly valued to this day.

With the invention in the 1820s of glass-pressing machinery, it became feasible to obtain inexpensive glassware if one could not afford the more costly hand-blown or cut glass. Indeed, one of the more famous of these early glass factories, the Boston and Sandwich Glass Company, led some people to refer to all early American glass as "Sandwich." Among the many items on which these artists impressed their great imagination were the "salts," or small containers for table salt, and the fancy cup-plates on which the cup was placed to prevent the marring of the table surface while hot beverage cooled in the saucer. American factories turned out pots, bowls, vases, tobacco jars, plates, cups and saucers, colanders, and shaving mugs; and jugs were made of earthenware and stoneware as well as glass, often highly decorated. In England there were craftsmen highly skilled in the making of porcelain, a material in which Americans eventually worked with great skill.

Painting

In order to make enough to support his family, the American artist had to turn to portrait painting, a genre that demanded that he work quickly and yet bring out the best features of his subject. He found it expedient to adopt the heroic or romantic tradition in order to avoid disappointing his client. Few mastered this style better than the famous American, Benjamin West; born to a Quaker family near Philadelphia, West "entered" Rome at ˙21, and went on to London at 24. There he was to assist in the founding of the Royal Academy and serve that institution as its second president. West spent most of his life in England, where he welcomed to his studio a host of aspiring American painters, among them Charles Willson Peale, formerly apprenticed to an Annapolis saddle-maker, who had been sent abroad to study by Baltimore businessmen on recognition of his talent. Peale returned to America after 2 years and began to paint portraits of George Washington, James Madison, Alexander Hamilton, John Adams, John Paul Jones, and others. To supplement his income he opened a museum of stuffed animals exhibited in display cases with backgrounds painted to represent the animal's natural habitat. Perhaps Peale's most charming painting is his *Staircase Group.*

Of his six sons, two became famous painters and appropriately bore the names of Rembrandt and Raphaelle. Rembrandt Peale studied with Benjamin West for a time; even more popular than his father as an artist, he painted a superb portrait of Thomas Jefferson.

Among the famous artists of the time was Gilbert Stuart, who also studied in West's London studio and is renowned for his many portraits of George Washington, one of which used to hang in many schoolrooms in the United States. John Trumbull, the son of the governor of Connecticut, was drawn to painting by his sister's needlework, the work of the artist John Copley, and lessons learned in the studio of Benjamin West. Perhaps his most famous painting is the *Declaration of Independence*, in which he depicted the faces of those present at the signing of that auspicious document on a canvas only 30 inches wide. Perhaps the leading artist of the time was Washington Allston, who graduated from Harvard in 1800 and then, on proceeds from the sale of an ancestral home in South Carolina, spent years in Europe learning his art. In 1819 he painted the beautiful *Moonlit Landscape*.

John Vanderlyn was sent by his patron, Aaron Burr, to Paris instead of London to learn to paint figures and the flesh. His painting of a nude in romantic setting, *Ariadne*, shocked his countrymen when it was exhibited in New York in 1815. Another artist, Samuel F. B. Morse, studied at Yale, and then with the encouragement of Stuart and Allston went to London to study with West. When he returned to the United States 4 years later he became one of the best portraitists, charging $15 a head. Morse always maintained that he disliked portraiture and did, in fact, spend much of his time working on larger canvasses, the most famous of which was his *Old House of Representatives*, painted in 1822. At the age of 41 he resumed his tinkering with electricity and invented the telegraph.

Thousands of artists who created interesting and unusually complex patterns, figures, and designs that rival anything produced by the so-called "op" artists of the twentieth century will be forever unknown, because most of their work has disintegrated or been destroyed. These artists were the women of the day who worked with needles, crochet hooks, patches, thread, yarns, and dyes extracted from available plants and vegetables to produce counterpanes, lace handkerchiefs, carpets, tablecloths, rugs, samplers, doorstops, pin cushions, chair covers, and patchwork quilts. Objects from their environment and their store of memories of objects became the decorative motifs of their needlework. Flowers, animals, sunbursts, farms, tools, birds, Bible verses, fruits, vegetables, cups, stars, waves, fish, and the very popular Federal eagle were reproduced and embellished in their art. The square, diamond, and triangle formed the basic elements of patchwork design, and they went by a thousand names—Dolly Madison's Star, Lemon Star, Missouri Puzzle, Coronation, Duck's-Foot-in-the-Mud, Mariner's Compass, and many others. It is a pity that so small a portion of this fine work is preserved in museums for the descendants of the artists to view and admire.

plans for systems of schooling

The American war is over; but this is far from being the case with the American revolution. On the contrary, nothing but the first act of the great drama is closed. It remains yet to establish and perfect our new forms of government; and to prepare the principles, morals, and manners of our citizens for these forms of government, after they are established and brought to perfection.

To conform the principles, morals, and manners of our citizens to our republican forms of government, it is absolutely necessary that knowledge of every kind should be disseminated through every part of the United States. Benjamin Rush althougth the Founding Fathers were in disagreement about the precise duties and responsibilities of the federal government, there was general acceptance of one important point. For the new republican form of government to succeed—and there was more than a little doubt on the prospects for its success—the people must have access to at least some formal schooling. The reason for this was obvious: in a system of government in which the citizens choose their representatives at the ballot box, the quality of that representation must depend on their ability to make intelligent choices; furthermore, since it is impossible for the voters to be personally aware of the qualifications and the political stance of all the candidates on the various issues, they must be able to read their candidate's published remarks and to make wise decisions on the basis of what they read, as well as what they are told. Thomas Jefferson, with his inimitable skill in the use of words, put it as well as it has ever been expressed: "If a nation expects to be ignorant and free, in a state of civilization, it expects what never was and never will be."

George Washington, perhaps the most revered of the Founding Fathers, devoted the major portion of his first message to Congress to the importance of education:

Nor am I less persuaded that you will agree with me in [the] opinion, that there is nothing which can better deserve your patronage than the promotion of science and literature. Knowledge is in every country the surest basis of public happiness. Whether this desirable object will be best promoted by affording aids to seminaries of learning already established, by the institution of a national university, or by any other expedients, will be well worthy of a place in the deliberations of the legislature.

Apparently the Senate agreed, at least in part, with the spirit of the president's remarks, since in its official reply of January 11, 1790, the Senate said:

Literature and Science are essential to the preservation of a free constitution; the measures of government should therefore be calculated to strengthen the confidence that is due to that important truth.

From the House of Representatives came the words: "The promotion of science and literature will contribute to the security of free government."

Among persons who gave careful thought to these matters, there were those who favored the promotion of education, but who looked in vain to the Constitution for an article that empowered the Congress to foster literary and scientific endeavors. The Tenth Amendment, even, was cited to uphold the view that in the absence of specific congressional responsibility, the matter of schooling devolved on the states or on the local governments. Still others believed that Congress bore some responsibility to aid education, but only if an amendment to the Constitution spelled out its explicit responsibilities in this area.

Whatever the argument that swirled around the relationship

of the central government to the nation's schooling, there was no question in the mind of the first president of the importance of learning to a free citizenry. In his Farewell Address he again bespoke his convictions as follows:

Promote, then, as an object of primary importance, institutions for the general diffusion of knowledge. In proportion as the structure of a government gives force to public opinion, it is essential that the public opinion should be enlightened.

What were the views of the other Founding Fathers? Benjamin Franklin for one, believed schooling could not save a corrupt civilization from inevitable decline, yet he was convinced that sound education was essential to a free and virtuous society. Franklin's fellow Philadelphian, Dr. Benjamin Rush, was one of the most ardent spokesmen on behalf of the importance of education. The American Revolution, Rush insisted, had not ended with the fighting at Yorktown. The form of government had been altered, he admitted, but much remained to be done to secure essential changes in "principles, opinions, and manners so as to accommodate them to the forms of government . . . adopted."

Along with a marked distaste for the encroachment of classical words and phrases on the English tongue, Rush was adamant on the need for the inculcation of republican principles in the youth of the expanding country. He denounced a European education as unsatisfactory for the new generation of Americans, even though he himself had studied medicine at the University of Edinburgh. What was needed in the new American republic was an education that would make the people homogeneous in sentiment and foster "a supreme regard to their country. . . ."

Rush expressed his views in a number of papers and speeches, perhaps the most notable of which was his "Thoughts upon the Mode of Education proper in a Republic." The young, he asserted, must be taught the superiority of the republican form of government, yet they must be made aware that constant efforts would have to be made to ensure improvements in men, in measures, and in the institutions of government.

In an article in the *American Museum Magazine*, Rush, while endorsing efforts to make education widely available, indicated his displeasure with the emphasis placed on the study of Latin and Greek at the higher levels to the extent of wishing to banish such words as *exit, fecit, excudit, acme, finish, bona fide, ipso facto,* and "a hundred others equally disgusting, from English compositions." He insisted, furthermore, that the English language must be preserved from the encroachment of such French and Italians words as *eclat, amateur, douceur, corps, dilettanti, piano,* and others that "impair the uniformity and dignity of the English language."

Science was to receive much greater attention, he asserted, because the prosperity of the country rested on rapid scientific development; indeed, one of the primary reasons that the mass of the people had little use for the colleges was that these institutions emphasized the study of the ancient languages and ignored practical matters. To Rush's way of thinking, natural history was extremely important as the "foundation of all useful and practical knowledge in agriculture, manufactures, and commerce, as well as in philosophy, chemistry, and medicine. . . ." Modern languages such as French and German would replace the ancient languages in Rush's curriculum; mathematics, history, logic, chemistry, philosophy, government, the principles of agriculture, and manufacturing were all to be included. Moral philosophy, often taught by the college president and regarded as the capstone of the educational experience because of its heavy concentration of theology and ethics, was to be replaced in Rush's scheme by "evidence, doctrines and *precepts* of the Christian religion."

Although he did not spell out all the details of his national system, Rush seems to have had in mind an arrangement of state enterprises. His plans for the state of Pennsylvania, for example, would have established free schools in every township with 100 or more families, a series of country academies, four state colleges, and a university "after the manner of the European universities." At the top of the pyramid, he envisioned a national university that would prepare civil servants for the central government. Of course, the university would be a creature of the government and it would be a place in which men were indoctrinated with "republican" principles as well as taught the skills needed by government officials.

Washington, too, believed in a national university and in his will set aside stock in the Potomac River Company worth about $25,000 should Congress extend "a fostering hand" to the university. In time the company failed and the shares became worthless; nevertheless, they gave evidence of Washington's belief that a national university might contribute to the success of the new government by ameliorating the sectionalism that threatened civil war. Among those who advocated a national university at one time or other were James Madison, James Monroe, Joel Barlow, John Quincy Adams, Samuel Smith, Samuel Knox, and Thomas Jefferson. Proposals for a national university put forth by Barlow, Smith, and Knox envisioned a university that would generate and disseminate new knowledge that would enrich the country; Benjamin Rush, on the other hand, bespoke an institution that would reinforce the principles of republicanism. It was as if the later advocates of the national institution assumed that knowledge would lead man inevitably to an appreciation of republicanism, whereas Rush and others thought it necessary to inculcate man with that appreciation.

Despite the nationalistic fervor of men like Benjamin Rush, Noah Webster did the most to modify European influences on American language and spelling. While eschewing personal vanity, he believed strongly in the need to nurture in Americans a national pride in their heritage, traditions, and future. His spelling books, especially *A Grammatical Institute of the English Language: Part I* (the "blue-back speller"), grammars, readers, and dictionaries—the most famous of which was the

American Dictionary of the English Language—and other works, all contributed to this end, and time and again he expressed his vigorous views on the proper relationship between these nationalistic aims and the educational process.

Education is a subject which had been exhausted by the ablest writers, both among the ancients and moderns, I am not vain enough to suppose I can suggest any new ideas upon so trite a theme as education in general; but perhaps the manner of conducting the youth in America may be capable of some improvement. Our constitutions of civil government are not yet firmly established; our national character is not yet formed; and it is an object of vast magnitude that systems of education should be adopted and pursued, which may not only diffuse a knowledge of the sciences, but may implant, in the minds of the American youth, the principles of virtue and liberty; and inspire them with just and liberal ideas of government and with inviolable attachment to their own country.

Like many of his contemporaries, Webster believed it more important to cultivate the "virtues of men ... than their abilities," and as the last sentence of the lengthy quotation above insists, a primary purpose of education should be inculcation of patriotism, an opinion shared, as we have seen, by Rush, Washington, and many of their fellows.

Not only Americans recognized the importance to the nation of the education of its youth; several European visitors to the United States recorded their observations on the importance of education as a reflection of the aspiration of the new republic. The Frenchman, Alexis de Tocqueville, who visited the United States from 1831 to 1832, observed the country and its citizenry with clarity surpassed by few writers in any day. His observations, no doubt, would have both delighted and saddened men like Noah Webster, because although he found Americans to have no monopoly on virtue, he reported the mass to be better educated than any other he knew. Moreover, asserted de Tocqueville, a majority of Americans possessed an understanding of public affairs, and "a knowledge of laws and precedents, a feeling for the best interests of the nation, and a faculty of understanding them . . ." unequaled in any other place in the world.

How many persons drafted plans for a "system" of education for the new republic is unknown, but there were many, among them, as we have seen, Benjamin Rush and Noah Webster. Thomas Jefferson's scheme for the state of Virginia, while not national in its scope, was to receive such widespread attention through the years that it is worthy of special note. In 1779, Jefferson and his friend George Wythe prepared for the consideration of the Virginia legislature A Bill for the More General Diffusion of Knowledge. Under this proposal, each county in the state was to be divided into parts called "hundreds" in a manner that would make it possible for each free child to attend school for at least 3 years without charge, and for a longer period if the parents could pay. Reading, writing, and arithmetic were to be taught, and in the course of reading instruction, the children were to learn some Roman, Greek, English, and American history.

In addition to the elementary schooling, there was to be a secondary system under which the state was to be divided into 20 districts with a grammar school in each constructed of brick or stone. Each school was to have several schoolrooms, a dining room, quarters for the master and his assistant, as well as 10 or 12 rooms for students. Money for these schools was to come from the public purse. Offerings were to include Latin, Greek, geography, English grammar, and higher arithmetic. Free schooling was to be made available to a few boys whose parents could not afford tuition, under the following arrangement. One boy to be selected among all those who qualified as "poor" at 10 elementary schools would attend grammar school free of charge. At the end of 1 year, a third of those so chosen were to be sent home. Of those remaining at the end of 2 years, only one was to be chosen to be educated at state expense for the remainder of the 4-year grammar school course of study. Finally, after 6 years of instruction, one half of the scholarship students (10 in all) were to be sent to William and Mary College to be instructed for 3 additional years at state expense. It strikes us today as unjust, this rigorous winnowing of the offspring of the poor, while the children of the more prosperous parents were permitted to continue their schooling as long as they could afford it. In fact, Jefferson's plan is often characterized as elitist, as, of course, it is when judged in the light of contemporary values. But then, we are all aware of the hazards in judging the events of the past by the standards of the present; in Jefferson's day, his plan may have been considered excessively philanthropic, or hopelessly naïve. Unquestionably, the plan was defective in allowing no provision for the education of the children of slaves, and little for that of girls. But, after all, it was a beginning, and there seems little doubt that had the proposal been adopted, Jefferson would have proceeded to expand and refine it. Indeed, Jefferson may have felt the scheme to be sufficiently daring without the inclusion of even more controversial provisions in the first draft.

However, it was the progressive spirit of the Wythe-Jefferson proposal that set it apart and made it worthy of study to this day. Embodied in its provisions were the ideas that education is the best means of preventing tyranny, that those people are happiest whose laws are best, and that good laws are made by wise and honest men, that in every society those persons whom nature has endowed with genius and virtue should be given a liberal education, regardless of birth, fortune, or "accidental condition or circumstance," so that they may be entrusted in time to guard "the sacred deposits of the rights and liberties of their fellow citizens. . . ."

In 1817, 40 years later, Jefferson drafted another piece of legislation, A Bill for Establishing a System of Public Education, which incorporated many features of the earlier bill. Unfortunately, neither was enacted into law, but were consigned instead to that scrap heap of dreams—some of them ingenious, others undeniably crackpot—that make up the "might-have-been" of history. Perhaps too few Virginia legislators were convinced as Jefferson was that "knowledge is power, that knowledge is safety, and that knowledge is happiness."

In 1818, the twilight of Jefferson's career, a special meeting was called at Rockfish Gap, Virginia, to consider establishment of a state university. The report that emerged recommended the founding of a university in Charlotteville, only 3 miles from Jefferson's home, Monticello, set forth the purposes of the new enterprise, suggested a curriculum, offered ideas for campus and buildings, gave estimates as to cost (seriously underestimating the total), outlined the duties of the "visitors" who were to direct the affairs of the university, and even detailed rules for student conduct.

To the delight of Jefferson the legislature authorized the university and the "Sage of Monticello," with the help of his friend, Joseph C. Cabell, spent many of the remaining days of his life working at the business of the university, often riding horseback to supervise the workmen erecting the beautiful structures he designed. Jefferson selected the site, surveyed it, designed the several buildings (instead of a single large one so as to avoid noise, "filth and fetid air"), pried money from the legislature, planned the course of study, the admissions requirements, the mode of governance, and even hired many of the first faculty men, who were eminent in their fields of scholarship, possessed of teaching ability, cultured, of high integrity, amiable, and imbued with the spirit of republicanism. No doubt Jefferson's concern for a faculty "imbued with the spirit of republicanism" could be interpreted as an attempt to imprint the institution with an orthodox political position, and so it was. Indeed, there were few persons so enlightened, or so foolhardy, as to knowingly employ on the faculty persons whose views were antithetical to those of their employers. In the twentieth century, legislatures, trustees, faculties, students, and the public examine the political views of professors from time to time; in the nineteenth century a teacher's political and religious opinions were also often matters of general concern.

Charles Eliot, who served as Harvard's president from 1869 to 1909, is sometimes referred to as the father of the elective principle—a curricular scheme that permits a student to choose all or a part of his courses. Jefferson permitted partial election in his curricular scheme for Virginia; he would not, he said, do as most other colleges of the time did, that is, hold all students to the same course of study. The university was to be divided into eight schools: ancient languages, modern languages, mathematics, natural philosophy, natural history, anatomy and medicine, moral philosophy, and law. All the various courses to be taught in these schools and other features of the plan as well give Jefferson's university the outline of the state universities that were to be created later that same century. An "academical village" was planned, with the students' rooms near those of the professors, partial election of courses, and advanced instruction in some areas; these and other features make one wonder what might have become of this "academical village" had Jefferson lived another 10 years; however, he died on July 4, 1826, when the college had been open less than 2 years. Although student disruptions at Virginia caused him great pain, the opportunity to create the university gave him great satisfaction in his last years. His epitaph, composed by Jefferson himself, declared that he was the author of the Declaration of Independence as well as the religious statutes of Virginia, and that he was the Father of the University of Virginia. And, in truth, he was.

It was probably no coincidence that in 1797, the year Jefferson and Rush served as the two chief officers of the American Philosophical Society, the organization offered a prize for the best plan for a system of education for the United States. Two winners, Samuel H. Smith and Samuel Knox, split the $100 prize money, even though the plan of neither was judged to be entirely satisfactory. Both Smith and Knox proposed systems proceeding from the elementary level to a national university, and both plans contemplated at least partial support from the public purse and vested responsibility for the entire system in a single board of control. Of the two proposals, however, Smith's is the more interesting in its details.

Not yet 30 when he composed his scheme for a national system of schooling, Smith had graduated from the University of Pennsylvania in 1787, and only 3 years later was the editor of the *National Intelligencer*, the official newspaper of the Jefferson administration. An enthusiastic public servant, he served as Commissioner of Revenue, president of the Washington branch of the Bank of the United States, and director of the Washington Library.

The Smith system comprised primary schools, colleges, and a university to be supported, in part, from a fund to be raised by a tax on property. All male children from five to eighteen were to go to school, and every parent was to see that his child either attended school or received a compensatory amount of instructional time at home. Each primary school was to have a student body of 50, divided into two age groups, five to ten and ten to eighteen. The younger children were to be taught English language, writing, and arithmetic and were to memorize certain passages in literature that taught moral precepts, described natural phenomena, or displayed "correct fancy." The older children were to learn higher arithmetic, the rules of English language, criticism and composition, history, geography, and the laws of nature useful in the practice of agriculture and mechanics. As their task of memorization, the older students were to be assigned the Constitution and the "fundamental laws of the United States."

Each year one boy was to be chosen from the advanced class to be supported at college at the public expense; of course, there was nothing to prevent the others from going on at their own expense. Each college was to have 200 students at work on advanced studies, including the "cultivation of polite literature." For the most diligent and talented, special opportunity was to be afforded at college so that they might pursue a number of "accomplishments," among which were modern languages, music, drawing, dancing, and fencing. From each graduating class, 1 student in 10 was to be admitted to advanced study at public expense in the national university. The entire system of education was to be directed by a 14-man board of literature and science with representatives from each of the following disciplines: literature, mathematics, geography and history, natural philosophy, moral philosophy, English, agriculture, manufactures, government and laws, medicine, theology, elements of taste (music, architecture, gardening, and drawing), military tactics, and "a person eminently skilled in Science, who shall be President of the Board." Members of the board were to hold office for life and to receive a "liberal salary, which shall render them independent in their circumstances." When vacancies occurred, the professors at the university were empowered to make recommendations for replacements, with final approval to be in the hands of the faculties of the colleges and the fellows of the university. The powers of this board would have included the selection of textbooks, the establishment of libraries, and the disbursement of cash prizes to persons who wrote superior articles on "subjects proposed by the board for discussion or such as shall make any valuable discovery." It was given responsibility, also, to examine all literary and scientific papers submitted to it, to publish the best pieces at public expense, and to reward the deserving authors.

To accomplish the aims of his educational scheme, Smith urged that partisan considerations be put aside in order to unite all good and wise men in the common cause. "Liberties," Smith cautioned, "depend upon the knowledge of the people and this knowledge depends upon a comprehensive and energetic system of education." The improvement of political institutions goes hand in hand with the development of mental resources; education fosters wisdom and virtue just as ignorance and passion breed discord and strife. Smith predicted,

The era is at hand when America may hold the tables of justice in her hand and proclaim them to the unresisting observance of the civilized world. Her number and her wealth vie with each other in the rapidity of their increase. But the immutable wisdom of her institutions will have a more efficient moral influence than her physical strength. Possessed of both she cannot fail to assume, without competition, the station assigned her by an overruling power.

Many writers and intellectuals of the day set down their ideas on the role of schooling in the Republic. Robert Coram, Nathaniel Chipman, Du Pont de Nemours, Lafitte du Courteil, James Sullivan, and others published extended essays on education or actually advanced schemes designed as full-fledged systems of national education. Extensive considerations of all proposals or plans need not concern us here, since many of them spoke in no special way to the needs of the United States. The student interested in examining the various plans will find that he can make a good beginning with two books: *Liberalism and American Education in the Eighteenth Century* by Allen Hansen and *Essays on Education in the Early Republic* by Frederick Rudolph.

Were all these proposals hopelessly utopian? Surely they were no more impracticable than the ideal of the republican form of government they were designed to serve. Indeed, a strong case could have been made—and was made—for the notion that the political experiment then underway depended for its viability on just such a systematic approach to the schooling of the nation's youth.

Just why one institution will survive when another succumbs is not always clear. In truth, the institution that failed in one era will be a resounding success in the next; the American university itself may be an example of this because its flowering occurred in the last half of the nineteenth century, not the first half. Still other institutions were never begun at all; instead they remained dreams or only words fading on yellow sheets of paper. One such was a plan for an agricultural college in Massachusetts; the report for it was drafted in 1825. The commission that prepared the report recommended a system of instruction in which the practical arts and sciences were to be stressed. The courses were to include French and Spanish, grammar, composition and rhetoric, bookkeeping and arithmetic, geography and history, drawing, mathematics, natural philosophy, geology, mineralogy, chemistry, agriculture and horticulture, moral philosophy, and political economy. The college was to have a farm of 50 to 100 acres; in addition to the usual lecture halls and recitation rooms, there were to be workshops in which students were to be taught common mechanical operations. Some of the students were to be prepared as schoolmasters. The plans for this college were remarkably similar to the schemes put forward years later on behalf of the land-grant institutions created under the Morrill Act of 1862. Another scheme that failed in 1831 in New Haven was a college for the education of black men.

If the idea of a system of schooling on a national scale was in keeping with the principles as well as the needs of a republican form of government, and if it was endorsed by so many prominent statesmen and leaders, the question remains, Why was none of these proposals implemented? The reasons are various and complex, and the truth must be sought from among a number of generalizations. Undoubtedly, many people who were favorably inclined to the idea of local control of schooling, and handsome support for that schooling as well, possessed strong reservations about federal meddling in the affairs of local schools, even to the extent of supplying badly needed funds by way of support. Indeed, in the early national period and later, the question of states rights versus those of the federal government was to occupy the thoughts of politicians and citizens alike.

Furthermore, the relationship between the survival of the political experiment in the United States and the quality of education of its people was not demonstrably clear to every-

one, despite the pronouncements of political figures, clergymen, schoolmasters, and foreign observers. At about the same
time that Samuel H. Smith was drafting his plan for a national
system of schooling, the British physician, Edward Jenner, was
demonstrating the power of vaccination to immunize patients
against the dreaded smallpox virus. The worldwide acceptance
of the vaccination principle reflected the widespread fear of
the disease and the understandable willingness to do almost
anything to avoid it. If Americans had had similar evidence
that a dose of schooling would have prevented the future instability in their government and institutions, they might have
paid more heed to the claims for a national system of education.
Later, when educational reformers were intent on building
more elaborate schools and colleges, the claims they would
make for formal schooling as a cure-all for social ills would be
almost as impressive as the claims made earlier for vaccination, although with perhaps less basis in fact. Most people,
however, were not persuaded that an elaborate system of
schooling would play a crucial role in the destiny of the Republic; on the other hand, such a system would undoubtedly cost
a great deal of money, certainly more than the amount needed
to support the existing town schools and colleges.

Still another difficulty all proposals encountered was the
traditional view of schooling as the proper domain of the
church or local authorities, the philanthropic agencies, and
most of all, the parents themselves.

One difficulty in assessing the relative popularity of any idea
that never really "catches on" is the fact that usually the oppo-
nents do not appear in full force until the proposal has received
wide publicity and perhaps is brought before a legislative body
for debate. Had a bill been introduced in Congress to create a
national system of education and then brought forth from committee for debate, the ensuing discussion might well have un-
covered impassioned opposition on several points. Surely any
analysis of the reasons for the apathy toward the various proposals for systematic, extensive nationwide approaches to

schooling must take into account the distaste felt by many for the word "national," with its implication of a central government usurping the powers of the people. The Founding Fathers were, in fact, revolutionaries who had thrown off the unbearable burden of a king and parliament they regarded as despotic; no wonder they were not anxious to put in its place a strong central government that might prove equally tyrannical.

There were other difficulties. As we have noted, under the Tenth Amendment all power not specifically delegated to the central government was reserved to the states or to the people; hence a national system of education would probably have required a constitutional amendment. Interestingly enough, there was ample precedent for the principle of federal support for education in, for example, the land ordinances of 1785 and 1787, which provided that a state entering the Union must set aside lands for schooling. However, the land ordinances, while reaffirming the traditional commitment of the central government to encourage support for education by means of land grant, still left details of the undertaking in the hands of the state and local authorities.

It is interesting to speculate in passing on the means by which the federal authorities would have set about instituting systematic formal schooling, especially on the frontier. The legal and political groundwork for a national system of schooling would have been challenging indeed.

Why these proposals were never implemented must, of course, remain forever as matter for conjecture, but many of the principles embodied in the various plans have been altered and expanded through the years, and will be changed and modified in the years ahead. The view that schooling was partly the responsibility of the state was by no means novel; neither, for that matter, was the idea new that government could be based on concepts of political and social equality. Furthermore, there was nothing startling in the idea that talent was to be found at all levels of society—among the poor and lowly as well as the rich and well-born—and that it was to the best interests of the state and the people to identify and support that talent whenever possible. Still, when these ideas were combined within the framework of a dynamic society dedicated, at least in theory, to equality of opportunity and possessed of a wealth of natural resources, powered by a people convinced of the virtue and value of hard work whose ranks were constantly swollen by others seeking a new life—and finding it—then one could expect exciting days ahead, days filled both with danger and achievement.

chapter six
schooling

The Americans are hardly more virtuous than others, but they are infinitely better educated (I speak for the mass) than any other people of my acquaintance ... the mass of those possessing an understanding of public affairs, a knowledge of laws and precedents, a feeling for the best interests of the nation, and a faculty of understanding them, is greater in America than any other place in the world. **Alexis de Tocqueville**

Financial Support

Twentieth-century Americans, accustomed to the channeling of massive sums into the educational enterprise by federal and state agencies, often find it hard to understand the public attitude toward schooling in the late eighteenth and early nineteenth centuries. The prevailing view reflected the fact that schooling had long been a concern of the churches, towns, and philanthropic groups, with some aid and encouragement from various levels of government in the form of charters, grants of land, special tax provisions, and the like. As a result, Americans of this era were not used to thinking in terms of a division between the public and private sectors in support of schooling.

Many questions were emerging, however, that would in time effect a fundamental change in attitude. If education was essential to the future of the state, if in Jefferson's words, it was important for "every man to judge for himself what will secure or endanger his freedom," and if the state alone had the requisite funds, then obviously education was a proper function of the state. But by which level of government was this function

83

to be discharged? The municipality? The county? The district? The sovereign states? The federal government? Or perhaps by all these agents in concert with private individuals and agencies? These questions still puzzle the people of this nation.

The beginning of the era also saw increasing popular support for the claims of formal schooling as a means of improving not only the individual and the state, but society as a whole. As we know, Thomas Jefferson, Benjamin Rush, Noah Webster, Benjamin Franklin, and George Washington were but a few who advanced this idea in one form or other. After the American Revolution, the United States had enjoyed cordial relations with France; the excesses of the Reign of Terror, however, cooled the ardor of many Americans who saw that, as one writer put it: "The hero of yesterday was regularly murdered by the hero of today; and the possession of the supreme control was only a regular introduction to the guillotine." But before encountering this disillusionment, Americans were singularly receptive to all aspects of French culture, including the writings of Voltaire and the theories of Jean Jacques Rousseau, as propounded in his influential books, *The Social Contract* and *Emile*. In *Emile* the author detailed his thoughts on the education of an imaginary youth, emphasizing the return to a state of freedom and nature as the basis for the eventual reform of a corrupt and tottering social order.

But before a society will support schooling, it would appear that a demonstrable relationship between the educational process and certain desirable societal and personal aims must exist. In the early national period, many people seem to have regarded schooling that went much beyond the elementary level as of dubious value except, perhaps, to young men headed for careers in the ministry, medicine, and law. And even these professions could be entered by means of a suitable apprenticeship. Certainly not everyone agreed that schooling was a good to be sought for its own sake. Jefferson, Rush, and Webster might envision a salubrious tie between schooling and the national destiny, but those about to enter a trade, farming, shipping, land speculation, or business saw sufficient evidence that fortunes could be made without benefit of advanced schooling. The main concerns of the people were economic, political, and religious in nature, and the connection between opportunities in these areas and the process of formal schooling, especially in the classical studies, was not altogether clear.

There were other constraints on support for schooling, as exemplified in the notion that too much schooling tended to implant noxious ideas in the brains of the young. Certainly the idea of sending children abroad to be schooled was abhorrent to many because of the danger of their imbibing antirepublican or aristocratic sentiments. And there were other misgivings. The educational enthusiasts, some felt, promised far more than they could deliver; furthermore, undue emphasis on the power of education and schooling to cure society's ills diverted attention from man's sinful nature as the son of Adam. Only by constant and intensive application of the truths of the Bible could the evil inherent in man be kept in check. Where, it was argued, would unrestrained desire for education lead except to the conclusion that all man's problems were essentially educational in nature, and that the logical solution was more schooling. The Presbyterian minister, Samuel Miller of New York City, saw the use of formal schooling to bring about reform as dangerous; to be sure, schooling was good, but in the hands of those who believed in such nonsense as the perfectability of man, schooling became a kind of panacea to which was attributed powers far beyond the means of any known educational approach; moreover, it became a false doctrine that diverted man from his proper efforts to search out the Divine Will.

Finally, no doubt there were a few in the United States, although perhaps not so many as in Europe, who believed that their education bestowed on them an elite status, and that expansion of the opportunity for schooling meant a concomitant expansion in the number who would claim higher social status.

Behind the abstract philosophic arguments as to the importance of an educated citizenry, however, was the inescapable fact that a free people must at least have the competence to read, write, and reckon. The next step, then, was to decide how to make schooling available to as many as possible. One means to this end was the allocation of some substantial and equitable portion of the public lands for the support of the nation's schools.

Even before the adoption of the Constitution, several states had ceded territories west of the Alleghenies to the central government. The disposition of these parcels of land and the remainder of the huge government land holdings known as the "public domain" was to be a matter of intense concern to settlers, land speculators, and politicians—not to mention the original Indian populations—for a century or more. The use of the public lands as a means by which to support public education was an old device even before the Revolutionary War, but there was a vast difference between the principle of federal and state *support* for formal schooling and the creation by the state or central government of a *system* of schooling.

When the Continental Congress enacted the Land Ordinance of 1787 (often referred to as the "Northwest Ordinance"), it committed to law the conviction that "religion, morality, and knowledge, being necessary to good government and the happiness of mankind, schools and the means of education shall forever be encouraged." In addition to reserving Section Sixteen in every township in the western territory for the maintenance of the public schools, the terms of the ordinance directed that there be set aside "not more than two complete townships to be given perpetually for the purposes of a university...." Truly, this was landmark legislation.

That same year the Constitutional Convention met in Philadelphia and produced a Constitution that made no direct provision for education. Nevertheless, there was some debate by Convention delegates on matters relative to education. For example, Madison and others proposed that Congress be given the power to create a national university, a move defeated by a vote of six states opposed to four states in favor on the grounds that specific provision for such an enterprise was unnecessary; congressional jurisdiction over the District of Columbia, it was argued, would empower the legislators to create such an institution without further constitutional authorization. This proposal and several others detailing specific activities of the federal government were defeated for several reasons, among them that ratification would be more difficult to secure for a Constitution laden with many specific and possibly controversial proposals than for a document speaking in somewhat more general terms of the powers of the central government. Later, when the Bill of Rights was added to the Constitution, the Tenth Amendment would declare that all powers not delegated "to the United States by the Constitution, nor prohibited by it to the States, are reserved to the States respectively, or to the people." Although there was still no explicit mention of education, many interpreted those words to mean that since control over the educational enterprise had not been delegated specifically to the Congress, it must reside with the States, and this view has prevailed for generations. However, support and control, as we have already seen, are by no means synonymous, even though at times the power to withhold support has, in effect, amounted to the power to destroy.

Attempts to secure public financial support for common schooling has had a long and intricate history, with progress varying from state to state. It has been traditional, when analyzing this phenomenon, to divide the nation into four parts—south, middle states, north, and west. Most areas, as Ellwood Cubberley pointed out, went through distinct stages in the movement for public financial support. At the outset, the schools within a state or region were still seen as the responsibility of private persons, the local churches, and the various benevolent societies. Later, the state provided words of encouragement (and little more) to those who wished to afford some formal schooling to the young; then it made grants of money to communities that set up their own school funds, and gave local authorities permission to levy taxes for the support of schooling. Eventually, minimum rates of taxation were set and tuition and fees struck down so that the schools were free to all. In time, funds for schooling came from state coffers and from the federal treasury.

It is important to recognize, however, that change took place slowly and at a rate that varied among the several states in the Union. Moreover, dozens of interesting financial anomalies could be cited; for example, schools have been supported at times by nearly every money-raising scheme known to man, including public lotteries, license fees, fines leveled against public drunks, bank taxes, rate bills (taxes on parents with schoolchildren), and the proceeds from the sale of prizes-of-war.

When encouraged by the Continental Congress to set up local systems of government, most of the states had adopted a constitution, although Connecticut and Rhode Island retained their colonial charters as adequate for the time being. In most of these state constitutions some provision was made for education of the young; however, the gulf between merely extolling the value of education and actually providing the funds necessary to build schools and to pay teachers was perhaps greater than it is in our own time. As a result, few of the state legislatures accomplished much beyond modest improvement of existing schools and some slight provision for the schooling of the poor. By the end of the eighteenth century about half of the 16 states in the Union had some reference to schooling in their state constitutions.

In 1784 the University of the State of New York was set up, and then in 1787 reorganized to give some modest direction to the schooling provided in that state. Later, in the early nineteenth century, under the administration of Gideon Hawley, who may have been the first superintendent of schools, and with the encouragement of George and DeWitt Clinton, New York had a school system, albeit a modest one, that resembled in its administrative details the French system of the time.

If legislation within individual states provides some clues to the rate of public school development, then, clearly, New England was the leader. In Massachusetts, tax support for schools had been reinforced in principle, at least, by a law of 1789, which required towns with 50 or more families to provide 6 months or more of common schooling, and towns with 200 or more families to have a 12-month grammar school for older children, as well. The small children were expected to learn to read, write, and work simple arithmetic, and to give evidence of "decent behavior." In the grammar school, the master taught Latin, Greek, and other subjects designed to enlighten his charges and to prepare them for college. It was the hope of local school committees that a college-trained master could be obtained, and for this purpose, a premium was often paid to secure the services of someone with collegiate credentials and the necessary letters attesting to his high moral character. Such persons were not always satisfactory, and consequently, many members of school committees harbored doubts about the quality of preparation afforded prospective school teachers by the colleges of the time. The more things change, the more they remain the same.

Unfortunately, the distance between legislative intent and its implementation and continuing supervision is widened when the state fails to take a hand and relies instead on the good will of local officials to see to it that the schools are "kept" in a manner that meets both the spirit and the letter of the law. In Massachusetts, for example, the law of 1789 authorized the formation of school districts that extended the authority of school officials from the towns to the surrounding rural areas, but it was not until later that these same officials were permitted to collect taxes to support the schools and to hold elections and meetings to decide school questions.

Opposition to tax support for local schools was common in the early national period, and powerful as well. Those who could afford to do so often sent their children to private institutions and were reluctant to pay taxes for support of schools that their own children did not attend. A common technique in the North for support of schools was the local school fund, augmented by periodic grants from state coffers. Both New Hampshire and Vermont created school funds and even set down guidelines for the development of school curricula, the qualities to be sought in teachers, requirements for building construction, and the like. Connecticut created a state school fund before the Revolution, using monies to be raised through the interest from the sale of public lands. In 1795 this fund was increased by more than $1 million from land sales in the Western Reserve in Ohio. Critics of this technique of raising money for the schools insisted that local officials tended to rely on these funds instead of pressing for heavier taxation, a charge to which there was some truth. In Connecticut, at least, the school fund enabled most children to learn some reading and writing if they lived within walking distance of a school. Children who lived farther away sometimes had to wait until they could sit a horse before learning to read and write. Incidentally, the desire of the Connecticut schoolmen to put a school within easy walking distance of most of the children of the state resembles the efforts of the community-college advocates in states such as Florida and California to put a community college within easy driving distance of most potential college students.

In New York State between 1795 and 1820 some progress was made in moving from an enterprise supported primarily with funds from private sources to one in which the private still dominated, but in which the state and city assumed more responsibility for the schooling of the young. Indeed, by 1820 New York City schools may have been almost as good as those in Massachusetts, with its much longer tradition of public educational effort. In 1795 a law gave some assistance to counties which were attempting to maintain schools. Later, a school fund was established, and in 1812 when the first permanent school law was passed, interest from the state school funds was given to those districts attempting to raise funds locally;

moreover, school officials were permitted to tax citizens to raise the necessary cash for the upkeep of buildings. This same law provided for a state school superintendent and later suggested requirements for teachers.

In Rhode Island, the idea of private control and support of schooling seems to have been quite strong. In 1800, the state passed a school law that was largely ignored, except in Providence, and repealed in 1803. Schools for the children of the poor were authorized in Newport in 1825.

Pennsylvania provided some schooling for pauper children from the public funds after 1802, but most schools were supported by one of the many religious and philanthropic groups within the state. Although agitation for public schooling came from several sources, including the workingmen's groups in Philadelphia, associations promoting the infant schools and manual-labor schools, and the Pennsylvania Society for the Promotion of Public Schools, it was not until 1831 that a school fund was created, and it was another 3 years before a system of state schooling was authorized. Even then the idea of public support for schooling aroused the ire of the various religious and ethnic groups in Pennsylvania, not so much because they opposed public education in principle, but because they wished to preserve their own language and culture and to control the schools they had been supporting out of their own pockets.

New Jersey's state school fund was created in 1816, and a few years later local school authorities were granted permission to levy taxes to support the schools. Delaware and Maryland also had laws creating school funds, and both attempted to provide some schooling for the children of the poor; for the most part, however, schooling in these states remained in private hands until after the Civil War.

Virginia, despite efforts of Jefferson and others, did not establish a school system until after the Civil War, preferring to rely on private tutors and on local schools supported by funds from public and private sources, with heaviest reliance on philanthropy, church coffers, and tuition fees. In 1810 the state created a Literary Fund that was used primarily for the schooling of the children of the poor. Later, in 1829, another such fund was created, this time for rural districts that wished to create free schools, but funds were so limited that little was accomplished.

In other parts of the South, including North Carolina and Georgia, school funds were created in the early national period, and efforts made, although with slight success, to secure legislation authorizing sound public schooling. In Georgia schools for poor children were opened in Savannah and Augusta, and by 1822 some money from the school fund was used to pay the tuition of poor children. In South Carolina, the city of Charleston was authorized to create a few charity schools, but little was done on behalf of public schooling until the post-Civil War era.

Farther west the move toward public support for schooling was augmented by the federal land policies set forth in the Land Ordinances of 1785 and 1787, in which lands were set aside for the support of schools and a university in each state. An Ohio law passed in 1821 permitted taxation for the support of the schools, but the enthusiasm with which town officials levied and collected these taxes depended on the attitudes toward schooling of the local citizenry. Communities settled by New Englanders who knew a tradition of some local taxation for school support seem to have been more inclined to accept the principle behind the public support of education. On the other hand, in areas such as Tennessee and Kentucky, settled by easterners who came from another tradition, it was more common to encounter reluctance to levy taxes aimed at supporting public schools.

Private Efforts

Fortunately, in the early national period, there was an increase in support for private educational endeavors. Many private colleges and academies came into being, and money from private sources was used to support elementary and charity schools in many states. Indeed, there was considerable truth in the assertion by Francis Wayland, president of Brown University, that the states had done not one tenth as much for education as had the churches of the various Christian denominations. He might also have cited the contributions of the various philanthropic and benevolent groups, such as the Free School Society of New York and the Manumission societies.

In some eastern cities—such as Albany, Providence, and Baltimore—private subscription societies were at work collecting money with which to finance the schooling of the children of the poor. The Society for the Free Instruction of Indigent Boys was active in Philadelphia, along with other groups such as the Association of Women Friends for the Relief of the Poor. New York had its Orphan Asylum Society and the Manumission Society, which sought to mitigate the "evils of slavery, to defend the rights of the blacks, and especially to give them the elements of an education." One of the most interesting of these associations was the Free School Society of the City of New York, founded in 1805 by businessmen and Quakers to provide schooling for children of the "unchurched poor." By 1813 the Society was receiving money from both the city and the common school fund of the state; by 1825 six schools were being run by the Society. Although nonsectarian, the schools provided their charges with instruction in the Scriptures as well as daily Bible reading, and the usual reading, writing, and arithmetic.

It is true, of course, that these private efforts to aid in the schooling of the poor failed to reach a very large number of children in the cities and fewer still in the rural areas; moreover, it can be argued that their effect was merely palliative, and consequently they delayed the general recognition of society's responsibility for the schooling of all its children, whatever the financial status of their parents. Nevertheless, the efforts of these well-meaning private groups was praiseworthy, and they represent a step, however faltering, on the road to widespread educational opportunity for all.

But whether supported by private or public agencies or both, the local schools in the early national period were certainly under the control of local authorities, even in those parts of Massachusetts where the term "local" encompassed the surrounding district as well as the town itself. It may have appeared to some, after the Revolution, that the new federal government, or at least the state governments, should manage the affairs of the schools; in fact, it was the local officials and committees made up of the city fathers, businessmen, clergymen, and other prominent figures who hired the teachers, paid the bills, collected the fees, and visited the schools from time to time to insure that lessons were underway, that the Scriptures were being read, and that deportment met community standards.

Innovations in Education

Whatever idealistic purposes war may be claimed to serve, however desirable the concessions to be gained from its successful outcome, its cost to formal schooling as to all areas of human existence is invariably disastrous. Schoolhouses make excellent buildings in which to quarter troops, young schoolmasters and the older male students make good soldiers, and the money that should be spent on the schooling of the young children is channeled into weapons and battle gear and the deploying of men to death on the battlefield.

The American Revolution left the schools and colleges of the nation, such as they were, in a sorry state. Yet all was not lost. Even during the years of conflict, events occurred that pointed to a surprising amount of intellectual vitality, and the optimist might even have found evidence enough to support the hope that when hostilities had ceased, substantial progress could be made in the education of the young.

One step forward was the creation of the literary society, one of the first of which was Phi Beta Kappa founded at William and Mary in 1776. It had chapters at Harvard and Yale by 1781, and eventually spread to other campuses. This society, and similar ones with their small libraries, discussion sessions, and debates, offered students in the colleges of the early national period some relief from the stultifying effects of the recitation and rote memory, much as the extracurriculum of today's college offers respite from examinations, lectures, and term papers. In time, Phi Beta Kappa became the scholarly society we know today, and many of the literary and debating societies disappeared altogether. But in those years in which they flourished, before the Civil War, they gave their members a chance to enjoy fellowship, and to read and discuss serious questions, especially contemporary ones so often ignored by faculties whose thoughts were riveted on the glories of ancient Greece and Rome and the hereafter.

Near the close of the early national period appeared the social fraternities that were to have such widespread popularity and to stir so much controversy on the American campus in the late nineteenth and early twentieth centuries. Among the first fraternities were three at Union College: Kappa Alpha, Sigma Phi, and Delta Phi, sometimes called "The Union Triad."

Another event that occurred during the Revolutionary War was even more significant in foreshadowing the coming changes in patterns of formal schooling. This was the establishment in 1778 of the Phillips Academy in Andover, Massachusetts. The academy movement will be considered in detail later, but it might be remarked in passing that eventually there would be 6000 of these institutions, which were the forerunners of the American high school and the massive secondary-education enterprise in the United States in the twentieth century.

Actually, a few "academies" had been established during colonial days in places such as Newark, New Jersey, Rockville, Maryland, Neshaming, Pennsylvania (1728), Prince Edward County, Virginia, Sugar Creek, North Carolina, Charleston, South Carolina, and Cherry Valley, New York. The Presbyterians were especially active in founding these institutions, which were part grammar school and part college. Usually aimed at preparing students for college, the early academies were, in a sense, less broadly gauged than their nineteenth-century counterparts, and, therefore, more like the older traditional Latin grammar schools. The word "academy" today often brings to mind a rather exclusive private institution, often with a high tuition and a college-preparatory curriculum; for some, the term also connotes a military training program. In the late eighteenth and nineteenth centuries—the halcyon days of the academy movement in the United States—the institution usually had a purpose broader than mere college preparation. Indeed, Benjamin Franklin, who is regarded by some as the father of the academy movement, was keenly interested in the "useful" studies, among them, modern languages, horticulture, "accounts," geometry, surveying, and "good breeding." Franklin and others opened an academy in Philadelphia in 1751, but it soon lapsed into the more traditional form of secondary education, the Latin grammar school, and within 4 years became the College and Academy of Philadelphia, an institution that survives today as the University of Pennsylvania.

A surprising number of other new schools and approaches to schooling came into being during the early national period in addition to the academies. To this day, 49 of the colleges founded survive; the professions saw schools of medicine and professorships in law added to existing colleges, and Judge Tapping Reeve opened his school of law in Litchfield, Connecticut. Engineering and increased emphasis on applied science marked the offerings at such institutions as West Point and Rensselaer Polytechnic Institute. Specialized schools were also established, such as Thomas Hopkins Gallaudet's American Asylum for the Deaf at Hartford, Connecticut in 1817. A gymnasium was opened in Boston in 1826 to provide instruction in physical activity, and the plans were drawn for a school for the blind in Boston in 1829. In this era, too, the Sunday school movement gained great popularity, and the Lancastrian or monitorial method enjoyed some vogue in the United States, Europe, and South America; there was warm interest, also, in infant schools for children of only two or three years of age. Attempts were made, too, to provide special schooling for Indian children, without much success, and for the children of free blacks in some of the larger cities such as Baltimore, New York, and Philadelphia. Toward the end of the period, in 1826, the first lyceum in the United States was founded by Joseph Holbrook at Millbury, Massachusetts. Within 20 years, several thousand local lyceums had been established in the United States to enable farmers, villagers, and townspeople to hear speakers who traveled a circuit discussing the issues of the day and to enjoy all forms of oratorical exhibitions and readings.

And there were changes in the curriculum. Bible verses and the moral precepts they were supposed to instill remained the staple of elementary schooling, along with reading, writing, and figuring, but gradually grammar, geography, and history were added. After 1800 the offerings of some of the academies began to include geometry, French, commerce, surveying, music, composition, and bookkeeping, as well as Latin, Greek, English grammar, geography, and arithmetic; a few academies offered an even greater range of subjects, especially those related to the arts of homemaking and agriculture. These curricular additions in the academies grew out of the realization that these new institutions must serve secular as well as religious ends; moreover, only a few graduates were destined for college, whereas, a great many would live out their lives as homemakers, apprentices, businessmen, farmers, tradesmen, skilled workmen, and shopkeepers.

In the colleges the curriculum expanded to include more history, modern languages, and science. The literary and debating societies, constituting part of what today we would call the extracurriculum, often provided students with fare more appealing than the offering of the college itself.

With the creation of the universities of Georgia, North Carolina, South Carolina, Michigan, Vermont, and others, the foundation was laid for the great expansion of state universities later in the nineteenth century. The University of Virginia was built in accordance with the plans of Thomas Jefferson, and offered a curriculum of his design that promised to go well beyond the classical studies so popular in most of the colleges of the day. Furthermore, the educational theories of Jefferson, only a few of which were implemented at the University because of his death shortly after the institution opened, foreshadowed the ideas behind the American research universities that would be championed at the end of the century by such men as Daniel C. Gilman of Johns Hopkins, William R. Harper of the University of Chicago, and Charles Eliot of Harvard.

Town Schools

A few of the larger towns had Latin grammar schools in which the dominant aim was to prepare a few boys for college; since the colleges required some knowledge of Latin, Greek, and arithmetic, the grammar school's offerings were determined for it by the colleges. Boys entered these schools—the most famous of which was the Boston Latin Grammar School—and spent the 6 or 7 years there reading arithmetic and Latin textbooks and studying the writings of Caesar, Ovid, Cicero, Vergil, and others. In the nineteenth century when college entrance requirements were expanded to include ancient history, geography, and higher mathematics, and later English grammar as well, the offerings of the Latin grammar schools were increased. Even before the Revolution, however, it was clear that the Latin grammar schools supported by both private and public funds were not appropriate for any but a few boys destined for college; as a result a few privately supported "English" schools appeared in which English instead of Latin grammar was offered, along with a variety of useful subjects designed to prepare a boy for a life in commerce and trade. These "English" schools were the forerunners of the academies and the high schools that appeared later in the nineteenth century.

However, the bulk of the responsibility for the schooling of American children rested on the town schools scattered throughout rural America. Because so much depended on the quality of the teachers in these schools, it is not easy to generalize about them; indeed, a change in teachers could render an excellent school dismal in 1 year. And a boy lucky enough to have had a succession of good teachers might find himself holding his own at Harvard or Yale in competition with graduates of the nation's best Latin grammar schools.

On the whole, we in the United States have tended to believe that there are really only two kinds of schooling—the good and the indifferent. But we must recognize still another—a third possibility: a kind of schooling that is so bad that it is antieducation, turning the young away from education or anything that resembles it or reflects its values. One wonders whether the latent antiintellectualism that is said to exist in the United States may not be the legacy, in part, of inferior schooling inflicted by a harsh schoolmaster or stupid schoolmistress. Accounts of schooling in the early national period were often concerned with the rapid changes of fortune within a school as the old teacher departed and the new one arrived. With so much depending on the qualities of the teacher, it is little wonder that school committees accounted themselves extremely fortunate to employ a teacher both learned and skillful with children.

Just as the schoolmaster might be either superb or incompetent, the quality of the schoolhouse in which he worked might be excellent or poor; from some accounts, it was more likely to be the latter. An unusually pessimistic view of school houses in New England was reported in the *American Annals of Education and Instruction*, Volume 7, for June 1837:

*With few exceptions [schoolhouses had] a single room, with
the chimney at one end, on one side of which was the door
and entrance.... There were generally no out-houses of any
kind whatever. Even the wood lay exposed to the snow and
rain. The furniture consisted of a chair, a table, a few benches,
and a writing desk; and the latter was usually attached to the
walls, on three sides of the room. The benches consisted of
slabs, with pegs for their support; and they were without
backs. The school room was in general so small that the pupils
were obliged to economize as much as possible in regard to
space, at the risk of crowding and jostling each other, and a
thousand other evils. This, we say, was the general state of
things.*

Not all descriptions of New England schoolhouses were as
gloomy as this; in fact, Timothy Dwight's descriptions were
glowing in their praise for those responsible for the maintenance of school property. But, in truth, Dwight often found
it difficult to restrain his enthusiasm for all things American.

Another description of a New England schoolhouse may
have been closer to the mean for those simple citadels of learning in the north. The Reverend Warren Burton attended the
same school in Wilton, New Hampshire, from 1804 until 1818,
and then went on to Harvard College and a career as a Unitarian minister. He started school at age three and one half in a
schoolhouse that stood at the top of a hill, with a woodpile in
back, and a broad, unhewn rock as a doorstep. The clapboard
siding was unpainted and the shutters protecting the six win-
dows were closed in the summer months to prevent damage
to the glass. Inside a pile of wood was drying, and a teacher's
desk sat on a raised platform to afford the occupant a clear
view of his charges ranged below. At the back of the room there
was a writing desk and a bench for the two oldest boys in
class. There was a fireplace and a closet in which garments and
lunch baskets were stored, along with the occasionally unruly
student. A half-dozen writing benches with seats were placed

in the middle of the room with lower seats for the very young. Usually the older the student, the farther back he was permitted to sit.

The school year was divided into a winter term, beginning in December, and a summer term, beginning in June. The older boys who were needed to help with farm work attended during the winter term and for a few days in summer when the weather did not permit outdoor work. This spasmodic summer schooling for the older boys, referred to as "rainy day schooling," did little good for the students and even less for the teacher.

The local school committee tried to secure the services of a male teacher—a college man if they could get one—for the winter term, and those of a woman for the summer. The succession of schoolmasters and schoolmistresses under whom the young Burton toiled was of uneven quality. One college student was one of the best teachers he ever had, and another was one of the worst. One master was so bad that the older boys threw him down an embankment and threatened him with stones and clubs should he ever return. It was the practice for schoolmasters to move from home to home, living with the families of their pupils for short periods of time during the term, and Burton remembered with pleasure the presence in his home of some of the schoolmasters.

Of the several techniques used to teach the young in schools, the recitation method was popular at all levels and in all places. Lessons were memorized and repeated before the class and teacher. Reading, writing, grammar, and arithmetic were standard fare; in addition, it was hoped that experience at school would reinforce efforts by family, community, and church in disciplining the intellect and developing strong character and purity of soul.

To assist them in the mastering of these lessons, students were provided with stories designed to instill good moral character. The famous story of George Washington and the cherry tree ("Father, I cannot tell a lie . . .") was reprinted in spelling books to encourage truthfulness. Diligence in the pursuit of the spelling lesson itself was the object of these inspirational lines:

> Joseph West had been told,
> That if, when he grew old,
> He had not learned rightly to spell,
> Though his writing were good,
> 'Twould not be understood;
> And Joe said, "I will learn my task well."

> And he made it a rule,
> To be silent at school;
> And what do you think came to pass?
> Why, he learned it so fast,
> That, from being the last,
> He soon was the first in the class.

The passage below was designed to guide an even wider range of behavior:

Love your brothers and sisters. Do not tease or vex them, nor call them names; and never let your little hands be raised to strike them. If they have anything which you would like to have, do not be angry with them, nor try to get it from them. If you have anything they like, share it with them.

Your parents grieve when they see you quarrel; they love you all, and wish you to love one another, and to live in peace and harmony.

Do not meddle with what does not belong to you nor ever take other people's things without leave.

Never tell an untruth. When you are relating anything you have seen, or heard, endeavor to tell it exactly as it was. Do not alter or invent any part, or make it, as you may think, a prettier story. If you have forgotten any part, say that you have forgotten it.

Persons who love the truth, never tell a lie even in jest.

The teachers' approach to discipline in the schoolroom varied considerably. Some used the rod heavily on the unruly, and, it would appear, on the ruly as well. Warren Burton recalled one teacher who insisted on absolute quiet in the schoolroom at all times, and would tie a child to his chair for an hour, twist an ear, or give a snap to the side of the head with a bethimbled finger for any childish turbulent behavior. Another teacher was over 6 feet tall and of such commanding presence that he seldom had any reason to dispense punishment.

For Burton and his colleagues, the last day of winter term was set aside for an examination in which the master put the students through their reading and spelling lessons. The school committee, a few parents, and the local clergyman appeared for the event. One year when the formal spelling exercise was ended, the clergyman asked if he could put a few words to the students. He chose words representing everyday objects seen in the home such as "penknife" and "andiron," words that were promptly misspelled. The lesson was clear; although the students could memorize the correct spelling for long words, they were still unable to spell relatively simple ones. When the writing books had been examined, the minister made a speech and offered a prayer; then the schoolmaster dismissed class until the next term.

The Lancastrian Method

Local authorities were always on the lookout for new methods of instruction, especially new techniques that would reduce costs. Of the several schemes put forth to educate the largest number with the least expenditure, few enjoyed the popularity of the "Lancastrian or Monitorial System," introduced in the United States about 1806.

In the Lancastrian System, popularized by the Englishman, Joseph Lancaster, small children were to be taught by older ones. The number of smaller children depended only on the size of the rooms built to house them and on the number of older children who were available to teach them. In other words, the Lancastrian approach gave to children who had learned a little the task of teaching other children who had learned nothing, and older children who had learned more were to teach those who had learned a little. Lessons were planned to ensure the careful monitoring of each step of the learner's progress. In a sense the planning was similar to "programmed instruction" of our own day. An elaborate system of rewards and punishment was devised, including candy for the responsive and placards for the inattentive, listing his shortcomings in print large enough for all to read. For a few, there were shackles. Lancaster himself is said to have devised methods for restraint and isolation that would bring immediate arrest of any teacher who used them today. The student teachers, sometimes called "monitors," were organized like a military unit, with older children in charge of younger ones and special monitors whose duties it was to see to the care of rooms and the distribution of school supplies. Old woodcuts of the Lancastrian school in Georgetown, District of Columbia, show an older boy with a pointer teaching geography lessons to seven younger children standing in a semicircle around him.

Joseph Lancaster came to the United States in 1818 to promote his system and was received with popular acclaim. Later, he went to Bolivia to set up his school, and returned to Philadelphia in 1827; he died in New York City in 1838, the victim of a runaway horse.

Despite its appeals to groups such as the directors of the Free School Society of New York who were trying, within a severely limited budget, to give some schooling to large numbers of students, the Lancastrian method was never as popular in the United States as in Europe; in Boston, which had some of the best schools in the land, it was never popular; for reasons not altogether clear the Boston newspaper men were never kindly disposed toward Joseph Lancaster. However, the method made some schooling available to those who might otherwise have known none at all. Shorn of its rather harsh punishments, it has a slight resemblance to "teaching assistant" programs employed in many American universities today under which young doctoral candidates receive a small stipend in return for instructing undergraduates. Like the Lancastrian method, these modern arrangements, at least in theory, make it possible for universities to offer instruction to many students at reduced cost; it also provides the teaching assistants with a little money without which they might be unable to remain in graduate school, and by sparing the professor introductory undergraduate teaching, frees him to work with more advanced undergraduates and graduate students.

Infant Schools

The infant school, promoted in England by Samuel Wilderspin and in Scotland by Robert Owen, was an attempt by these enlightened men to give some instruction in reading and writing to children of three years and older who would be denied the chance for advanced schooling later when they would be obliged to work 12 to 13 hours a day in factories. In the United States, a few cities such as Boston, New York, and Philadelphia established infant schools to prepare children for entrance to the local schools. In time these were absorbed by the town school systems.

Sunday School

The Sunday school was another import from England. Its original intent was to teach some reading and writing to the children of the poor, who roamed the streets of the cities on Sunday with nothing to do until it was time for them to return to the factories on Monday morning. Robert Raikes, a printer from Gloucester, did much to popularize the movement in England, and by 1786, Sunday schools modeled along English lines opened in Hanover County, Virginia, and later in South

Carolina. In 1790 the Methodists formally recognized the Sunday school as being worthy of encouragement, and by 1830 the idea had spread to all the eastern states and many western ones as well. Sunday school societies spread from denomination to denomination until 1824, when they joined in loose federation to found the American Sunday School Union. In the best tradition of the American organization, the Union issued a report in 1830 announcing that there were 5901 Sunday schools in the country. Reading and writing and other simple lessons as well as the catechism were taught the children of the poor and others who wished to attend. Unusually vigorous in the South and middle states, the movement enjoyed considerable popularity in Massachusetts, where by 1826 there were perhaps 22 schools and 400 teachers. The Sunday schools were housed in church buildings; it was the practice among the Presbyterians, Baptists, Episcopalians, Methodists, and others in Philadelphia to place "pious young ladies" in the corners of their churches, each of them to teach 20 to 30 children some Bible verses and some reading and writing. In Hartford, Connecticut, an "African Sabbath School Society" was organized to provide a Sunday school for the children of poor blacks.

At first the Sunday school functioned as a primary school for the children of the poor with a little Bible study thrown in for good measure, but as the public schools improved and reached more children, the Sunday schools became more specialized, until their function was exclusively religious. Attempts to secure public monies for the support of these schools had met with some success; however, because the churches were among the best organized of the institutions interested in charity work, it is not surprising that the Sunday school became their special province. How much good the Sunday schools did remains a matter of conjecture; however, a little schooling is probably better than none at all, and if only a few benefited from the teaching provided by the Sunday school, the movement must be considered a success.

Special Schools

Other schools of the period included the "African Schools" for black children in cities such as Baltimore, Philadelphia, and New York, and the mission schools for Indian children, such as the one conducted by the American Board of Missions at Cornwall, Connecticut, and others supported by public money, such as the school at Brainerd, Massachusetts, which was attended by both Indian and white children. A school for the deaf and dumb was opened in 1817 in Hartford, Connecticut, by Thomas H. Gallaudet, with the assistance of a society dedicated to helping the physically handicapped. A year later there were 50 pupils enrolled. In Boston in 1829 plans were laid for a school for the blind, but the first students were not admitted until 1832, about the same time that similar private institutions were opening in New York and Philadelphia.

The Academies

Of all the institutions that proliferated in the United States in the early national period, none was more interesting than the academy, an institution that seemed peculiarly well suited to an energetic people with unheard of resources of land and natural wealth—a people determined to get on with the job in hand.

Benjamin Franklin was as instrumental as anyone in promoting the idea that the Latin grammar school alone could not meet the needs of the American people. The advertisement for his academy, which appeared in the Pennsylvania Gazette in 1750, proposed course offerings in no less than 24 subjects and promised that more would be added. Yet the school in Philadelphia that Franklin championed never lived up to his expectations and quickly departed from the original intent of its founder.

The real burst of enthusiasm for the academy came after the Revolution and probably reached its zenith in the 1820s. In

1778 the Phillips family had created an academy in Andover, Massachusetts, and later founded one in Exeter, New Hampshire. Pennsylvania had York Academy, and North Carolina and Virginia both had academies named Liberty Hall. As we have seen, an older form of the academy, more limited in scope, had preceded even these; the Presbyterians had established several academies even before the Revolution. By 1820 much of the schooling beyond the elementary level was provided by the various academies that had sprung up to replace the town Latin grammar schools, even in Massachusetts, where the grammar school was required by law in the larger towns. In time the academy was replaced by the public high school, but in the decades between the Revolution and the Civil War, and even for some years thereafter, the academy was the queen of the American secondary education enterprise.

The variations among the academies was even greater than among the secondary schools of today, since the term encompassed institutions that were the equivalent of the Latin grammar schools as well as log cabin enterprises "about twenty feet square, with a doorway cut out of the logs . . . ," a rough door hung on wooden hinges, a chimney of logs with red clay mortar plastered over them, and a 3-inch plank that had been adzed until it was more or less smooth and fitted with wooden legs to serve as a desk for everyone.

The academy differed from the public Latin grammar school and the public high school in that it was organized by private persons or groups. In the South, as one might expect, the various denominations—the Methodists, Baptists, Quakers, Presbyterians, and others—were unusually active in creating academies. There were distinct advantages in the early national period in being a private instead of a public institution. For example, charters were easy to obtain—often there was no requirement other than the payment of a modest fee—and there was little or no supervision by the state or other agency. The holders of an academy charter would design almost any curriculum they thought desirable and required the presentation of admissions credentials as relaxed or as strict as they wished. Furthermore, appeals for funds could be made to private donors, to churches, to municipal officials, and to state legislators. An academy in Leicester, Massachusetts, for example, apparently took advantage of all these sources, obtaining a building and land from private benefactors, money from the town coffers, and private donors, and additional lands from the state legislature. Unlike the public institutions, which were dependent on the good will of a citizenry that still had unpleasant memories of what it regarded as the excesses of British taxation, the private institutions took what they could from the public purse and were also able to draw on private sources. In time, of course, as the distinction between public and private would be drawn with much greater precision, the private institutions would have to depend more and more on private sources for their financial support.

Theodore Sizer, who studied the growth of academies in the United States, reported that there were at least 6000 such institutions by the middle of the nineteenth century. In the North were the Deerfield Academy, the Academy of Marblehead, the Westfield Academy, and an academy in York County, Maine, which opened in 1791. One of the earliest academies was Dummer Academy in Massachusetts. Norwich, Vermont, was the home of the American Literary and Scientific Academy founded by Captain Alden Partridge in 1819. By the end of the eighteenth century, Virginia alone may have had as many as 25 academies; by the middle of the nineteenth century, the state could count perhaps 200 more with charters, and still other unchartered institutions. North Carolina had about 30 academies before the end of the eighteenth century. Among the academies in Georgia was the Richmond County Academy. Little Rock Academy was chartered in 1825 in what is now Arkansas. In New Orleans in the early nineteenth century, a plan was proposed for creation of a university of New Orleans, which was to supervise the activities of a college as well as a network of academies, including schools for girls. The whole scheme, which was later abandoned, was to be supported by a combination of lotteries and appropriations.

Accompanying the rapid spread of the academies was an increase in the number of colleges; as many as 500 were created before the Civil War, of which about 174 survive to this day. Indeed, it was often hard to differentiate between some academies and the smaller colleges; and, in time, a good many academies attained collegiate status. For example, Liberty Hall Academy became Washington and Lee University, and Prince Edward Academy in Virginia became Hampden-Sidney College.

Although the academies prepared students for college, they also prepared them to enter business and trade; the girls were trained in the arts of homemaking, but their education did not stop there. The founders' statements are rich in their references to the importance of science and literature, and to the desirability of studying the ornamental as well as the useful. Some of the larger academies had literary and debating societies similar to those in the colleges. At Exeter the Golden Branch Society boasted a library that rivaled those of many of the small colleges of the time.

Theodore Sizer maintains that the offering and purposes of many academies were broader and more various than those of the early high schools; indeed, he suggests that the academy may well have been more closely attuned to the needs of the last century than the high school that replaced it was. To be sure there were academies that were little more than one-man operations set up in rented facilities for as long as the tuition money held out; there were other "academies" that left as their only records the yellowing advertisements placed in forgotten newspapers.

Since many academies were boarding schools, parents had to have the money to pay for both tuition and board and room. Despite the money brought in from tuition, teachers in the academies were of uneven quality and usually were poorly paid. By all accounts one of the best teachers of his time was a black man, John Chavis, who had studied at Washington

Academy and was an ordained Presbyterian minister. In his school in Raleigh, North Carolina, he taught white youngsters, many of whom later became prominent in the affairs of the state. Attached to this operation was a school for the sons of free blacks, an institution that probably did not survive the laws restricting the opportunities of both slaves and freed men in the 1830s.

The curricula in many academies were surprisingly broad, although whether they were much broader than the skills and knowledge possessed by the teachers, one can only surmise. In the larger institutions, Latin and Greek were offered along with English grammar and literature, algebra, rhetoric, and surveying; French was often popular, as were United States history, bookkeeping, composition, geometry, arithmetic, geography, and many other subjects. A report to the New York Regents of the University of the State of New York listed Latin, Greek, English grammar, geography, and arithmetic as being offered in 50 academies in the state. Some academies, the report continued, had as many as 30 subjects on the books. At the end of the early national period some of the larger academies were offering to both boys and girls courses designed to prepare them for teaching in the common schools and the academies as well. With perhaps as much as nine times as many students in academies as in college by the middle of the nineteenth century, the demand for teachers was far greater than the colleges could supply, even if they had been willing to do so, and the academies therefore had to carry much of the burden of supplying teachers for the lower schools.

In addition to academies offering a wide range of courses and studies, a number of specialized institutions developed. In the South, for example, there was much interest in the military academies, which taught military discipline, marching, and the wearing and care of the uniform, along with the usual dosage of Latin and arithmetic. A flurry of interest in the advantages of manual labor as a part of the education of the young occurred in a few academies late in the period, perhaps as a result of the Pestalozzian-Fellenberg movement in Europe. The basic premise in these institutions was that manual labor was a salutary part of the educational experience because it contributed to health, morals, habits of industry and thrift, and simultaneously provided the student with a useful skill. A few went so far as to insist that manual labor would encourage independence of spirit and reinforce the principles of republicanism. Some who rejected this claim asserted that athletics would accomplish almost as much and at less cost. The prospectus for a Fellenberg school at Windsor, Connecticut in 1824 announced many of the courses of study found in other academies, but added that an attempt would be made to "adapt the studies to the capacities of each scholar, and to the course of life to which he may be destined." Emphasis was to be placed on the practical knowledge of the sciences, with particular attention to bookkeeping, chemistry, botany, and the sciences related to agriculture. Apparently a farm was to play a major part in the education of the young because the students were to be given a chance to engage in "agricultural pursuits." The purpose of the school was to prepare young men for the "more active employments of life," but they were also to have an opportunity to prepare for college.

From the creation of the "English Classical School," later known as the English High School, in Boston in 1821, some have traced the origins of the American high school. Recommended by a school committee of prominent citizens, this public secondary school opened with an enrollment of 102 students and the intention of preparing students not only for college but also for the "active life" and the professions, whether they were "mercantile or mechanical." Only boys were admitted at first, but in 1826 the High School for Girls opened with 130 students, and, in time, even the graduates of that school headed for college as well as the "active life."

Despite the claims of the English Classical School, the real roots of the public high school of the nineteenth century lay in the private academies, institutions that offered an ambitious program of studies for young people preparing to assume their roles in a vigorous society.

Education for Girls

Many voices in the early national period deplored the limited opportunities for schooling available to girls and young women. Most girls had to be content with a little skill in reading and writing; the luckier ones attended an academy, where they could achieve a certain proficiency in mathematics, Latin, French, embroidery, music, history, and composition.

Historically, a few religious groups acknowledged women as the spiritual equals of their brothers, but seldom did that equality extend to matters of schooling. Opportunity to enter the professions did not begin to approach that available to young men, nor were females admitted to apprenticeship or to the colleges.

In towns such as Boston, the wealthy retained tutors to instruct the children of the family, including the girls, in music, dancing, good manners, embroidery, sketching, and similar "accomplishments." These parents also took pains to give their children the confidence and sophistication that was thought to accompany travel and the reading of novels. Critics of these attempts at cultivation and refinement saw the acquisition of "accomplishments" as often harmful, especially if its aim was to give the child a little skill and knowledge that would win admiration at fashionable salons and garden parties. "With this education," said Timothy Dwight, "what can a son or daughter become? Not a man nor a woman; but a well-dressed bundle of accomplishments. Not a blessing nor an heir of immortality; but a fribble or a doll." Doting parents, the critics insisted, were to blame for making "accomplishments" the means, rather then the end; and what was particularly deplorable, the girls, who were given too little academic training as it was, were bound to assume that pretty dresses and pretty manners would avail them more than hard thought and disciplined action.

The serious deficiencies in the education of girls were remedied to some extent by the opening of academies that admitted both sexes and by the founding of special "female seminaries," such as that begun by Emma Willard in Middlebury, Vermont, in 1814 and the Troy Female Seminary (Emma Willard School) in 1821. To those seeking broader educational opportunities for women these new institutions must have represented the dawning of a new age. These special schools trained girls in domestic, literary, and religious matters, as well as in mathematics and philosophy. An academy in Ipswich, Massachusetts, announced that "in the manner of instruction, the principal object will be to excite a spirit of inquiry to lead the pupils to think and to investigate for themselves." An unusually ambitious academy in New Haven planned to offer work in geography, elements of composition, exercises in elocution, use of the globes, history of the United States, ornamental penmanship, algebra, astronomy, stenography, chemistry, Greek, fine needlework, natural philosophy, flower and velvet painting, music, and 32 other subjects.

Opportunities for women at the collegiate level were few until the establishment of women's colleges later in the century. Wesleyan Female College of Macon, Georgia awarded degrees to women in 1836, and Oberlin admitted women to collegiate study the same year. Mt. Holyoke Seminary in Massachusetts (1837) and North Rockford College for Women (1849) were among the largest of the women's colleges. Later in the century, the growth of the normal schools and the state universities brought more and more women into the ranks of the student bodies. Photographs of nineteenth-century student groups suggest that these young women took their new opportunities seriously; invariably, their demeanor is dignified and their backs ramrod straight as they peer in the camera's lens with expressions rendered even more severe by hair neatly drawn back from a center part. Long after women had been admitted to colleges on a coeducational basis, the belief persisted that serious study was unfeminine, that it encouraged women to rise above the station for which the divine will had intended them, and that the mingling of the sexes in an educational setting would result in a confusion of the roles and attributes of both men and women.

Tutors

The young lad of promise who showed a marked ability in the mysteries of Latin, the intricacies of arithmetic, and the profundities of theology might come under the wing of the local clergyman for special instruction in languages and theology in preparation for college entrance. Not surprisingly, his aim was often to follow in his mentor's footsteps. If he were a poor boy, he might be provided with a modest scholarship by the local parish or philanthropist, with the understanding that when his studies were ended, he would return to minister to the spiritual needs of his home community. Some young men found it necessary to augment their funds by taking time off from their studies to serve as schoolmaster or as tutors in wealthy families. In time, some even became discouraged with the prospects of the clerical life and devoted themselves to professional teaching instead.

In the south the tutor was an important personage in the plantation "family," standing just below the local clergyman, and a cut above the local physician and lawyer—that is, of course, if he were a gentlemen, and not an indentured servant, and if he knew his Latin. Before the American Revolution the wealthy southern planter sometimes sent his children to England to be educated, a practice that declined in the postwar period because of increased costs and misgivings as to the dangers that anti-republican ideas might be implanted in the minds of the impressionable young. Instead, the planter was more apt to employ a tutor and donate money to the coffers of the local church. The church, in turn, maintained the local church school for a few months of the year, and employed someone—the clergyman's wife, a traveling tutor, or an educated indentured servant—to offer instruction. If the tutor served a single family, he was given a room in the plantation house or a building nearby in which to meet his charges. What was learned under these schemes, of course, depended on the energy, imagination, and learning of the tutor, as well as the inclination and wit of the pupils.

Professional Schooling and Apprenticeship

Young men who wished to become lawyers, physicians, or engineers might attend a college to learn their professions. In the United States professors of medicine were to be found in some American colleges, such as Harvard, Philadelphia, Dartmouth, Yale, and Columbia. A few Americans, among them Benjamin Rush, went abroad to study medicine at the University of Edinburgh. The aspiring lawyer could study with one of the few professors of law in an American college of the day, or he could attend Judge Tapping Reeve's law school in Litchfield, Connecticut. A third course was to study abroad, perhaps at London's Inns of Court, long famous for the preparation of English lawyers. In the field of engineering, the United States Military Academy at West Point soon became known for the quality of the work performed by its graduates. This fame survives to this day in the Army Corps of Engineers, which supervises a good many engineering projects in the United States and elsewhere. Another institution to gain fame from the work of its graduates in the design and construction of factories, shops, and mills, as well as other engineering efforts, was Rensselaer Polytechnic Institute.

Founded at Troy, New York, in 1824 by one of the great patroons, Stephen Van Rensselaer, the institution was fortunate to have as its first president the botanist and geologist, Amos Eaton. Students studied surveying, physics, manufacturing, gardening, agriculture, chemistry, and engineering, everything, in short, that touched on "the diffusion of every useful kind of knowledge, with its application to the business of living." They learned by teaching fellow students, by conducting experiments, and, later, when the ban on it was lifted, by listening to lectures. The laboratory method, the field trip and, above all, the study of the practical were emphasized, and students visited mills and workshops and studied nature at first hand. This most remarkable institution foretold the coming of both the industrial and agrarian revolutions in the United States, as well as the founding of the state land-grant universities that were to provide the opportunity for advanced schooling to children of industrial and farm workers.

For the most part, however, future lawyers, physicians, and other professionals, not excluding many clergymen, took the road to their professions through the land of apprenticeship. The doctor-to-be persuaded a practicing physician or surgeon to let him serve as his assistant and then followed him on his rounds, learning to use such tools as the lancet and the bleeding cup. He might also spend some time in an apothecary's shop learning the mysteries of remedies, herbs, potions, and drugs. The prospective lawyer might work as a law clerk, delving into law books and observing the ways of the profession; some merely read a little law and then hung out their shingle. It goes without saying that professional standards were poor, tragically so in medicine. For a long time, college students pursuing the regular academic curriculum, many of whom intended to enter the ministry, looked with disdain on fellow students intent on the pursuit of medicine, science, and law. President Philip Lindsley of the University of Nashville is reported to have said in his inaugural address in 1829 that it was easier in Tennessee to qualify for the practice of medicine and the law than for the shoeing of a horse.

Artists and architects learned their skills by studying with a professional; as we know, an impressive number of American artists worked in the London studio of Benjamin West before returning home to try to earn a living painting portraits and landscapes. In the ranks of American professionals, especially among architects, were to be found a number of European immigrants who had come to the United States in search of opportunity or to escape their oppressors, and in some cases, both.

The boy who wished to become master of his own ship served first aboard a ship as cabin boy and later as midshipman. In time he might work his way up through the officer ranks to the command of his own vessel. Navigation skills were acquired under the tutelage of the ship's master and by assiduous study of that remarkable book on navigation, *The Practical Navigator*, by Nathaniel Bowditch.

As a rule, one learned surveying from a practicing surveyor, although Abraham Lincoln is a notable example of one who acquired this skill from a schoolmaster with a little knowledge of the subject. This and other specialized skills were sometimes taught by private-venture teachers who promised to impart the mysteries of their technical knowledge for a price. Someone with ready cash could avail himself of the services of such teachers by responding to an advertisement placed in a newspaper.

To become a blacksmith—always an important figure in every American town and village, and on most plantations as well—it was customary to work as an assistant to a skilled practitioner of that trade. The same was true of the leatherworker, tinsmith, silversmith, wheelright, miller, glazier, and boatwright. The young apprentice to a blacksmith, for example, would grasp with tongs the pieces of red-hot iron drawn from the forge while the blacksmith applied his hammer. By watching his master at work the boy learned how to shape iron, temper it, and then apply the iron to a wheel or a plow or a horse's hoof. If his master were gregarious, he and his apprentice might halt their labors late on the autumn afternoon to enjoy mugs of crock cider and to discuss the issues of the day with clients and neighborhood idlers.

The rigors of apprenticeship were not unknown to men who

later achieved notable success in life. One of the most famous Americans to serve an apprenticeship was Benjamin Franklin, who was taken from school at the age of ten to help his father, a tallow chandler and soapmaker; 3 years later he was apprenticed to his older brother, a printer. Another famous apprentice was Andrew Johnson, seventeenth president of the United States, who was apprenticed to a tailor at age fourteen and ran away 2 years later.

Colleges

Yale College and most of the other eight colleges founded in the colonial era were closed from time to time during the Revolution, their buildings commandeered to house troops and stores, their students and faculty under arms, and their equipment stored in private homes until the threat of war was removed. With the restoration of peace, the era of college founding began in earnest. The number of colleges that are still in operation was to double in the first two decades after the Revolution, and to double again in the following two decades; other institutions opened their doors only to close them again in the years preceding the Civil War, but the net result was a 20-fold increase in the number of colleges that survive to this day, in a period that saw only a 10-fold increase in the country's population.

Why so many colleges? As with any complex phenomenon, only a combination of factors can provide a satisfactory explanation. As Americans pushed westward, Ohio's population soon exceeded that of Virginia and many of the older states in the East. The difficulties, dangers, and expenses of travel led Ohio settlers to establish colleges near at hand so that their children would not have to return to the East for their schooling. Then, too, regional and denominational rivalry played an important role in the proliferation of American educational institutions. Each religious group was reluctant to depend on colleges founded by other denominations for fear of having its future clergymen indoctrinated in the tenets of a rival belief. Congregational clergy educated at Harvard, for example, could not be expected to serve adequately the needs of a church of Presbyterians. And if members of a particular denomination were uneasy about the proselytizing of their future ministers, they had even more misgivings about exposing their own children to the teachings of another religious sect.

Still other forces for the establishment of colleges were the pride of community released by the Revolution, the peculiarly American pursuit of "progress," and the steady migration to the West. If eastern towns had colleges, then western towns must have them too. Moreover, charters were easy to secure; anyone might "found" a college whether or not he had the necessary resources. As a result, new institutions quickly met financial disaster, and a substantial number were colleges in name only.

What was the nature of the colleges in the early national period? They were absurdly small. It was not until after the Civil War, for example, that Harvard had a graduating class of 100. Harvard graduated only 47 in 1827, the year in which totals for several other colleges in the north were as follows: Bowdoin, 32; Dartmouth, 38; Vermont, 14; Williams, 31; Amherst, 23; Brown, 38; Yale, 79; Union, 68; Columbia, 34; Pennsylvania, 15. In all of New England in the early nineteenth century there were probably less than 1000 students attending college out of a total population of about 1½ million. In 1810 the ratio of college student to the total population was about 1 in 1500; today, the figure is 1 in 30.

Although Latin, Greek, mathematics, and moral philosophy —the "classical studies"—with a heavy theological overlay continued to dominate the curriculum of the colleges after the Revolution, important changes were underway. Here and there chemistry, physics, and mineralogy were introduced in addition to "natural philosophy." At Yale, philosopher-turned-scientist Benjamin Silliman permitted students to watch and even assist him as he conducted chemical experiments in basement rooms. Sometimes modern languages such as French and German were accepted as substitutes for the traditional Latin and Greek; at Union College, under the remarkable Eliphalet Nott, who served as its president for almost 63 years, the so-called partial-course program was introduced. Under this arrangement, a student could substitute French for Greek and elect some courses. By 1828 the "parallel" program at Union was perfected, permitting more mathematics, science, and modern languages in place of some of the traditional Latin and Greek. The study of political economy was introduced at several colleges in the late eighteenth century, as were many other small, although significant curricular changes.

In 1812, Yale College, with an enrollment of 313, had six tutors, five "academical" professors, and three professors of medicine. The "academical" professorships were in theology, law, mathematics, natural philosophy, chemistry, mineralogy, languages, and ecclesiastical history. The medical professorships were in anatomy and surgery, in the theory and practice of "physic," and in materia medica and botany. By the end of the early national period the three professional schools of the medieval university—medicine, law, and theology—had their counterparts, albeit modest ones, in the United States. The College of Philadelphia had a medical school about 1765, Harvard Medical School was organized in 1782, and by 1812 the size of the Harvard medical professoriate was almost as large as that for the rest of the college. Yale had a school of medicine by 1813, and professors of medicine were employed at Dartmouth, Brown, Vermont, and other colleges.

Law schools seem to have developed more slowly, although professors of law could be found at Columbia, Pennsylvania, Maryland, Transylvania, and elsewhere. One of the most famous professors of law, George Wythe at William and Mary, was an admired teacher of Thomas Jefferson. Harvard opened a law school in 1817. The first law school, however, seems to have had no college affiliation at all. Instead it was the handiwork of Judge Tapping Reeve of Litchfield, Connecticut, who in 1784 undertook to train students wishing to enter the legal profession. Among the prominent alumni of this "school" were Horace Mann, John C. Calhoun, and Aaron Burr, all of whom studied the law both as a system of rules and as a set of problems in practical jurisprudence. To enhance the precision with which legal problems would be solved by the fledgling lawyers, a moot court was created before which the students could "practice" the arts of oratory so important to the career of the successful counselor-at-law. Apparently several generations of young lawyers-to-be studied Blackstone's *Commentaries on the Laws of England* and Kent's *Commentaries on American Law.*

With its heavy emphasis on religion, the college of the colonial and early national eras seemed to some to have been as much a theological school as a "liberal" arts college. Indeed, testimony to the "liberating" influence of religion is often to be found among the writings of those who praised the classical studies. Furthermore, many graduates of these colleges, although fewer, perhaps, after the Revolution, were headed for careers in the ministry. There is said to have been concern over the fact that Jeremiah Day, a professor of mathematics, was not an ordained clergyman at the time he accepted the presidency of Yale College. The consternation aroused by this circumstance was allayed by his ordination before the inauguration. With the establishment of the Andover Theological Seminary in 1808, however, it became possible for the Congregationalist, at least, to attend a professional theological school run according to the tenets of his own religious beliefs.

Harvard College in 1812 had a few more professors but fewer students than Yale; there were seven "academical" professors, seven medical professors, and three tutors, one to teach Latin, another to teach Greek, and the third with responsibility for geography, geometry, astronomy, and natural philosophy. The library, with 15,000 volumes, was not only the largest possessed by any college, but probably also the best, although then, as now, size did not guarantee quality.

Most of the colleges in the United States were smaller than Yale or Harvard. Williams had 95 students, a president, a vice-president, a professor of mathematics and natural philosophy, two tutors, and a library of 1000 volumes. Most colleges of the time had a building, although few were as large or as well built as Brown University's four-storied, brick structure, which was 150 feet long and 46 feet wide. Brown was unusual, too, in the stipulation that its 36-member board of trustees was to include 22 Baptists, 5 Quakers, 5 Episcopalians, and 4 Congregationalists. Dartmouth was begun by Eleazar Wheelock as an academy dedicated to the education of Indian youths, and it even aided with the schooling of Sampson Occum, an Indian who became a prominent preacher and missionary. However, Dartmouth did not pursue this mission for long, possibly because the Indians preferred their ancestral ways to those of the white men, and their fathers were similarly disenchanted with schooling that taught little in the way of hunting skills, endurance to cold and hunger, physical prowess, and all the other arts and skills essential to the Indian's way of life. Not only did they fail to offer instruction in the Indian tongue, they taught languages unused even by the white man himself.

The colleges were supported by funds from many sources, among them tuition, church donations of land and money, and legislative appropriations. Most if not all the institutions founded in the United States before the nineteenth century, and many founded later, received money from the state governments. Brown, M.I.T., Yale's Sheffield Scientific School, Dartmouth, and Rutgers were among the beneficiaries under the Morrill Land Grant Act of 1862, which did much to stimulate the founding of public colleges in this country. In time, of course, when the distinction between public and private colleges became more finely drawn, the money from the state legislatures began to dry up.

As we know, Yale was one of the largest of the colleges at this time, with three four-story buildings, each with 32 rooms, for "academic" pursuits. In addition, there were a chapel, a laboratory, special quarters for professors, a library, and a home for the president. First-year students studied the literature of Rome and Greece, geography, and mathematics. The second year they continued these studies and added some English grammar and history. In the third year there was a text on natural philosophy to be mastered along with some astronomy, chemistry, and more history. The fourth-year student studied logic, more chemistry and natural philosophy, the writings of John Locke, and moral philosophy and theology. Every Sunday a sermon was preached by the professor of divinity, and from time to time the professor of law gave lectures on the law, the Constitution of the United States, and the jurisprudence of Connecticut.

First-, second-, and third-year students recited before their tutors two to three times a day, while the seniors recited once a day to the president. At lectures the students took notes and were examined on what they retained from the previous lecture. Compositions were written from time to time by all students, and the juniors and seniors conducted "disputations" on questions assigned by the teachers.

The bachelor's degree was awarded to successful candidates after an examination of the senior class by professors, tutors, and others invited to the college for that purpose. After a lapse of 3 years, the holder of the bachelor's degree might apply for his master's degree. There were no formal course requirements as a rule, but a fee was exacted and sometimes a master's paper was submitted along with evidence that the applicant had stayed out of jail in the interval.

A student found to be deficient at a regularly scheduled examination might be degraded or put back a year in his study. (This practice, until recently, at least, was still employed in some professional schools in the United States.) If a student broke the rules of the college—and there were a great many to be broken—he would be admonished the first time; a repetition of his errant behavior would elicit another warning, this one brought to the attention of his parents. A third transgression earned dismissal, which made it impossible for him to be readmitted without the favorable vote of the entire faculty. Other forms of punishment were employed, such as whipping, public admonishment, often at chapel, and rustication, that is, being sent home for a time or to the parish of a country clergyman for the correction of erroneous ways by a strict man of God. The following bit of doggerel warns of that awesome prospect: "Let me warn you, sir, beware, lest you smell the country air." All these forms of punishment and others were used in one college or another.

Life at Harvard was similar to that at Yale. Admission requirements were comparatively easy to meet for the boy who knew his Latin and Greek grammar and a little mathematics. The common method of instruction, the recitation, required that the student memorize the content of his textbook and repeat it to his tutor. Student progress was measured, therefore, by ability to memorize. Of course, when the recitation was treated more as a question-and-answer session, it could, in the hands of a skillful teacher, resemble a Socratic dialogue, but unfortunately, it was seldom used in this way. Long prayers offered in the early morning and evening in drafty chapels and dining rooms contributed little to the intellectual excitement of the colleges. In truth, as the Englishman Abijah Weld observed on seeing Princeton and other colleges of the time, the higher institutions in America were really not much more than grammar schools. He described their libraries as wretched things poorly arranged and stuffed with old books on theological topics. At one end of Princeton's library, Weld observed two small cupboards that contained "a couple of small stuffed alligators and a few singular fishes in a miserable state of preservation, from their being repeatedly tossed about."

Placed in or near small country towns far from contaminating urban influences and built on a hilltop to avoid the fetid air and to afford an inspiring view of the countryside, and, perhaps a closer proximity to heaven, these institutions packed into dormitories and classrooms young men with the juices of youth coursing in their veins. They were lonely places for the fifteen-year old away from home for the first time, surrounded by other striplings, taught by a system of memorization and recitation designed to exercise the mind by tutors and professors ready to stamp out signs of the devil's handiwork. Little wonder that college students were about as ready to riot over some real or imaginary grievance as they were to be converted by a visit from a revivalist preacher at the end of a long winter. Under so paternalistic a system students often resorted for amusement to such turbulent behavior as roasting a turkey obtained by stealth and the consumption of spiritous liquors. (It is said that there were rooms at Harvard known as "the tavern" for 20 years after the departure of the occupant who earned for his quarters that interesting appellation.) Part of the difficulty lay in the belief held by many college officials that the youths in their care must be carefully protected and disciplined if they were to resist the temptations of the flesh and the spirit. The clergymen-teachers who supervised students had their thoughts fixed not on the petty concerns of the present, but on eternity. Their charges, on the other hand, were young and less introspective; the pursuit of immortality had less appeal for them than the experiences of the day.

One of the results of this rigid authoritarianism was riot. Bad food, a dispute between student and teacher, or merely the zephyrs of spring could provide the spark that touched off disturbances ranging in intensity from a little broken glass to death for the participants. At Princeton in 1807 over half the student body was suspended. After a rebellion at Harvard in 1818 the young Ralph Waldo Emerson was rusticated for a few weeks to contemplate the evil of his ways. In 1830 Yale experienced the "bread and butter rebellion." Later there was the "conic section rebellion," so called because it was brought on by student refusal to recite certain mathematics lessons in the manner prescribed by the teacher. The difficulties experienced by the University of Virginia in the 2 years after its founding caused keen anguish to the founder and chief architect, Thomas Jefferson. At Harvard on one occasion, over half the senior class was expelled. Among those who tried to soften the strict rules of student conduct and to appeal to the scholar's better nature were Eliphalet Nott of Union and Timothy Dwight of Yale, who said he believed that if the student were treated as a gentleman, he would act like one, at least on most occasions.

Another interesting outlet for student enthusiasm, although not so newsworthy as the riot, was the literary and debating society that became popular in the middle and late eighteenth century at William and Mary, Yale, Harvard, Princeton, and elsewhere. Intercollegiate sport, which drained the hellish physical energy of the participants and the equally hellish emotional energy of the observers, was unheard of, and organized athletics of any kind were rare indeed. Even the attempt to transplant the German *turnverein* with organized tumbling and gymnastics was not highly successful in these colleges. With the exception of some of the academies, coeducation was untried; hence, in the colleges even the moderating influence of women was absent, if, indeed, women do constitute a moderating influence.

Most colleges were host to two literary and debating societies. At Princeton there were the American Whig and Cleosophic Societies, at Brown the Philerinenians and the United Brothers. Membership was often determined by the student's political sympathies; indeed, these societies probably owed their existence to a combination of the aridness of collegiate life and the burning contemporary political issues of the eighteenth century, issues that were in the thoughts and on the lips of every informed citizen and filled the pages of pamphlets, newspapers, and magazines.

The search for an ancient or modern equivalent to the activities of these groups reveals that they had in some degree the appeal of the public disputation found in the medieval university, something of the eloquence heard in the oratory of the Indian council circle, and a bit of the skill of advocacy learned in the moot court of the modern law school. In addition, however, the societies reflected something of the respect for the powers of reason and intellect championed by Voltaire, Diderot, and his fellow Encyclopedists, although it would appear that a clever classical allusion was often prized more highly in debate than a telling fact.

Complete with constitutions, elected officials, and libraries that were sometimes superior to those of the colleges in whose rooms they met, these societies gathered regularly each week (Saturday afternoon was popular) to debate a series of questions devised by a committee created for that purpose. Debate was usually conducted by a team of speakers, with opportunity provided for general comment at the end. When all was finished, the winners would be declared. Among the questions debated by the United Brothers at Brown in 1818, for example, were these: "Would a union of the two parties which exist in the United States, which are known by the name of Federal and Republican, at present be justified?" "Have the Protestants of Europe a right to combine and destroy the Inquisition?" Needless to say, the last question was decided in the affirmative. Inevitably, perhaps, these societies, dealing as they did with contemporary political and social issues, would become involved in public disputes. The Phi Beta Kappa Society at Yale, for example, had several public controversies with those who believed in the principles of Jeffersonian republicanism, a doctrine regarded by many members of the society as heretical or worse.

Commencement week was always an important time for the literary and debating societies, because that week represented the climax of the academic year both for the societies and the college as a whole. Furthermore, since most colleges had two or more societies, there was a natural battle for supremacy among them. The weapons used in this war were usually words, as members of the society and prominent alumni as well would be invited to read poetry, give orations, and debate. To the delight of small boys, a few societies would sponsor a parade complete with brass band and drum. In 1786 a notice in a newspaper announcing the forthcoming commencement exercises at Harvard warned:

To the ladies:
The students of Harvard College present their respectful compliments to the ladies and beg leave to inform them, that as the present mode of wearing balloon hatts is attended with disagreeable effects in public assemblies, they have voted to admit no lady into the meetinghouse on commencement day, whose hatt shall exceed the breadth of 15 inches. They can also dispense with hoops of an immoderate size ... N.B. The doorkeeper will be furnished with a measure.

In time, the activity that had been the chief concern of the literary and debating societies became an integral part of the college itself as those institutions made an attempt to be contemporary. As this happened, the societies disappeared.

However, in the 1820s at the end of the early national period, another society began to develop—the fraternity—that endures to this day, although its relative strength is not what it was only a few years ago. Beginning about 1826 at Union and Hamilton Colleges, the fraternity seems to have been both a reaction to the harsh college life itself and an expression of the continuing need of the young to associate with one another without the restraining influence of their elders, to share interests and secrets, pledge loyalties, and to enjoy the pleasure of social life. In time, the fraternities built small libraries just as the literary and debating societies had done. They elected officers, secured quarters in which to conduct their secret rituals, and even sponsored their own debates. Almost from the beginning, fraternities were subject to tirades by college presidents who saw in their secret rituals purposes antithetical to those of the college, antidemocratic tendencies, and potential for conspiracy. Despite attempts to outlaw fraternities or through better dormitory design to render them redundant, an uneasy truce was reached. Today their imposing structures, identified by the appropriate Greek letters, still line the tree-shaded streets near many campuses.

Dartmouth College Case

In the early national period changes were occurring in the curriculum of the college. Modern languages, for example, were being introduced at Miami of Ohio, Ohio University, Harvard, Vermont, Amherst, and elsewhere. At Union College the "parallel" course of study was evolved that permitted the substitution of modern languages and science for some of the traditional work. But despite the efforts of reformers, the traditional collegiate ties with a religious denomination were retained along with the classical curriculum emphasizing Latin, Greek, mathematics, natural philosophy, and moral philosophy taught by means of the recitation with a few lectures interspersed. The faculty was still heavy with clergymen, who emphasized character building and soul saving.

Two events of the period—the Dartmouth College case and the Yale Report—symbolize the power of the older ways of conducting college business. In 1816 the legislature of New Hampshire, which was dominated by the Jeffersonian Republicans, attempted to take over Dartmouth College and convert it to Dartmouth University under state control. After the discharge of President John Wheelock by the trustees of the college, a series of charges was brought against the institution, including the accusation that it had begun to harbor certain aristocratic tendencies. The trustees of the college took the case to court in the Superior Court of New Hampshire and lost; the college, it was ruled, was a public corporation subject to the control of the legislature. Meanwhile there were two colleges operating side by side with separate trustees, faculties, and students. When the case was appealed to the United States Supreme Court the trustees were lucky enough to secure as their attorney the eloquent Daniel Webster, himself a Dartmouth graduate. In a plea that lasted for hours, Webster closed with the following moving appeal on behalf of his alma mater:

This, sir, is my case. It is the case, not merely of that humble institution, it is the case of every college in the land. It is more. It is the case of every eleemosynary institution throughout our country ... the case of every man who has property of which he may be stripped—for the question is simply this: Shall our state legislature be allowed to take that which is not their own, to turn it from its original use, and apply it to such ends or purposes as they, in their discretion shall see fit? Sir, you may destroy this little institution ..., but if you do ... you must extinguish, one after another, all those great lights of science, which, for more than a century, have thrown their radiance over the land! It is, sir, as I have said, a small college, and yet there are those that love it. ...

The Court's opinion for the five to one majority overturning the decision of the New Hampshire court was written by the federalist and Chief Justice John Marshall, who declared that Dartmouth was a private eleemosynary institution and not a public institution under public control. Long a case cited in support of private property, the Dartmouth College decision clarified to some extent the distinction between public and private institutions—a distinction that was unclear in 1819 and is not entirely clear to this day. Moreover, by erecting a partial shield against undue interference from public officials, the case gave impetus to efforts to establish private colleges. Furthermore, it strengthened the hand of those, the trustees, holding an institution's charter. The Dartmouth College case said, in effect, that if states wished to create colleges, they would have to do so *de novo* or secure the permission of those holding the charter for an independent college to do so. But what is most important of all, the case tended to remove the private colleges to a short distance outside the political arena where they would not be subject to the ebb and flow of political tides. What was more, the protection given the private colleges tended, in part, to benefit the public colleges as well. A curious result of the case, which perhaps could not have been foreseen, was that the separation of the public from the private could work to the detriment as well as the benefit of the private institutions. As the danger of political interference diminished, so, too, did the right of access to the public purse, which had long been an important source of revenue for private colleges. In time the state coffers would close to the private institutions, including Dartmouth College.

The Yale Report

A second major event of the early national period that attests to the strength of the traditional colleges in the United States was the publication in 1828 of the Yale Report. This document was a defense of the traditional way of conducting collegiate affairs and of the classical curriculum, which was dominant in colleges of the day and was destined to remain so until late in the nineteenth century.

As we have noted, Yale's graduating classes in the 1820s were the largest of any American college, exceeding even those of Union and Harvard. Known as the "mother of faculties and presidents," Yale was eminent among the institutions to which other colleges, especially western ones, looked for faculty and presidential talent. It was understandable, therefore, that a report prepared by the president and professors of Yale College should arouse keen interest in the educators of the time. Its publication by Benjamin Silliman in 1829 in his periodical, the *American Journal of Science and Arts*, assured it a wide circulation, and the report was read as have been few such documents since.

Professor James L. Kingsley and President Jeremiah Day seem to have had heavy responsibility in the writing of the Yale Report, which was a defense of the college as it had been, and, for that matter, as it would be for several decades to come. The theory of learning it supported was "faculty psychology," or the notion of the mind as both a receptacle for worthwhile knowledge and a muscle to be strengthened by exercise. "The two great points to be gained in intellectual culture, are the *discipline* and the *furniture* of the mind; expanding its powers, and storing it with knowledge." The process of enlightenment was not a simple one, however; reading a few books, listening to a few lectures, "or spending some months at a literary institution" would not suffice. Subject matter appropriate to this discipline was to be drawn from the ancient studies. Mathematics would teach the art of reasoning; science would enable the student to become "familiar with facts, with the process of induction, and the varieties of probable evidence." Ancient literature provided "finished models of taste." Logic and philosophy would teach the art of thinking, rhetoric and oratory the art of public speaking. Composition would teach "copiousness and accuracy of expression." Extemporaneous discussion would enable the student to become "prompt, and fluent, and animated."

The report also defended the use of lectures and the recitation method by which students memorized the contents of textbooks and then repeated them daily to their tutors. The argument on behalf of this course of studies resembles the claims made for general education a century later, except, of course, in the content of the course offerings. "Our prescribed course contains those subjects only which ought to be understood...by everyone who aims at a thorough education." French and German were offered at Yale, the authors of the report insisted, but only in the nature of "accomplishments," not as necessary acquisitions. The report also chided the critics of American higher education who urged the establishment of universities by advancing the hope that Yale would not make the ludicrous mistake of attempting to imitate the German universities until such time as adequate funds were available. Answering the critics' demands for education in practical affairs, the authors upheld the classical course of study as affording the newly affluent the judgment and wisdom as well as the liberal views that would ensure their enlightened use of wealth and power. The skills of the counting room must be learned in the counting room.

With its powerful defense of the *status quo*, the Yale Report made it clear that the institution and others that subscribed to principles expressed therein would continue to serve the few and not the many.

Textbooks

In 1783 President Ezra Stiles of Yale College predicted that a common language would be one of the forces to bind together the diverse elements of the American experiment. If Stiles was right, then Noah Webster, the lexicographer and music teacher, must be credited with a major contribution to the prospering of the United States.

Webster's *A Grammatical Institute of the English Language: Part I*, later known as the *American Spelling Book* and *The Elementary Spelling Book*, was published the same year the president of Yale offered his prediction. To millions of children who used it (as many as 70 million copies may have been sold), it was known simply as the "blue-back speller" (even though it was not always bound in blue). There were other spelling books on the market, but none enjoyed the popularity of the "blue-back" with its stories and lessons in morality as well as word lists and guides to pronunciation and spelling. Later, Webster published a grammar and reader that included a little history under the title *An American Selection of Lessons in Reading and Speaking* (1785). Over the years these books saw many revisions. In 1828, Webster brought out what is perhaps his most famous work, the *American Dictionary of the English Language*.

Textbooks in science were rare and usually written for use in the college classrooms. Benjamin Rush's *Syllabus of a Course of Lectures on Chemistry* (1770) enjoyed some popularity. In 1808 Benjamin Silliman of Yale edited William Henry's *Epitome of Experimental Chemistry* for use by advanced students, and in 1830 he published his own book, *Elements of Chemistry*. An Englishwoman, Jane Marcet, was the author of *Conversations on Chemistry*, reprinted in the United States in 1809 and used in teaching the rudiments of science to younger children. Books on geography were also rare, but Jedidiah Morse, the father of the painter and inventor Samuel F. B. Morse, published notes he had taken as a student at Yale College under the title *Geography Made Easy* (1784). Nathaniel Dwight, brother of the president of Yale College, was the author of *A Short But Comprehensive System of the Geography of the World: By way of Questions and Answers. Principally Designed for Children and Common Schools*. An example of the questions is: What is a gulph? The answer is: A gulph is a large bay. Near the end of the era, atlases supplemented geography texts that sometimes were fairly accurate in depicting the domain as far as the Mississippi River; beyond the river, however, they remained mostly blank, and the little information available about the West was often inaccurate.

One of the most popular history texts ever written was the work of an unusually enterprising textbook publisher, Samuel Goodrich. *Tales of America*, published in 1827, featured a white-haired old man named "Peter Parley" who suffered from gout and entertained young listeners with tales of Indian raids, wars, and other events in which he himself may or may not have been an active participant. Goodrich's titles sold more than 10 million copies and were justly famous for their excellent woodcuts. Lexicographer Joseph Worcester also wrote a few histories for schoolchildren.

Surely one of the strangest texts ever inflicted on the American schoolchild appeared in 1815. Written by R. T. Hunt in the style of the King James version of the Bible, one passage read as follows:

Now it came to pass, in the second month of the same year in which David gat home to the United States, that the armies of the north began to be in motion, and departed from the place called French Mills, where they were encamped.

The popular *New England Primer*, later versions of which ran to about 100 pages of alphabet, vowels, syllables, verses, and couplets with woodcut illustrations, was still popular in the nineteenth century; however, many other primers were in use, some of them named after the city in which they were published, for example, the *New York Primer*, the *Boston Primer*, and the *Albany Primer*. Among the readers available was Webster's *Grammatical Institute of the English Language, Part III.* Another, entitled *The American Preceptor*, was written by Boston schoolmaster Caleb Bingham and was intended to teach moral precepts as well as reading. Bingham also wrote a grammar with the delightful title *The Young Lady's Accidence* in 1785; it was studied by Warren Burton in his clapboard school in New Hampshire. Another text popular in both the United States and Britain was *English Grammar*, written by Lindley Murray. For students of Latin, there was Peter Bullion's text, *Principles of Latin Grammar.*

Nicholas Pikes's *New And Complete System of Arithmetic* appeared in 1788; another popular arithmetic book of the early nineteenth century was *Schoolmaster's Assistant*, by Nathan Daboll. And there were many other books on oratory, penmanship, elocution, and the like.

Whereas city children had a few texts over which to drowse, children on the frontier usually had to make do with the Bible, the "blue-back speller," and perhaps an almanac. Of the libraries in 1800, Noah Webster said, "We have not such things. There are no more than three or four tolerable libraries in America and those are extremely imperfect."

In a society in which the molding of character and the welfare of the immortal soul were matters of grave import, it is not surprising to find great care exercised in the selection of poetry and prose for inclusion in the readers, grammars, and spellers. If there was a choice to be made, it was invariably based on pious sentiment instead of literary merit.

Few books and periodicals designed to aid the teacher appeared before 1830. Two periodicals enjoyed brief publication and then folded: *The Academician* (1818–1820), published in New York, and the *American Journal of Education* (1826–1830), printed in Boston. A popular text used in training teachers was Samuel Hall's *Lectures on School-Keeping* (1829).

Epilogue

As a reflection of the essential role foreseen for education by the enlightened men of the early national period, and as a reminder to us in the twentieth century of what must yet be achieved before the United States can fulfill the destiny envisioned by its founders, these words by Samuel Harrison Smith, written in 1796, cannot be bettered.

No truth is more certain than that man will be happy if he can. He only wants a complete conviction of the means to pursue /that end/ with energy and success. This conviction the United States may be destined to flash on the world....

Many of the most enlightened of our citizens will traverse the globe with the spirit of philosophical research. They will carry with them valuable information and an ardent enthusiasm to diffuse it. Its diffusion will be the era of reform wherever it goes.

But more important, still, will be the example of the most powerful nation on earth, if that example exhibit dignity, humility, and intelligence. Scarcely a century can elapse before the population of America will be equal and her power superior to that of Europe. Should the principles be then established, which have been contemplated, and the connection be demonstrated between human happiness and the peaceable enjoyment of industry and the indulgence of reflection, we may expect to see America too enlightened and virtuous to spread the horrors of war over the face of any country and too magnanimous and powerful to suffer its existence where she can prevent it. Let us, then, with rapture anticipate the era when the triumph of peace and the prevalence of virtue shall be rendered secure by the diffusion of useful knowledge.

a brief selected bibliography

a student interested in the development of schooling and education in the early national period will be pleased to find a number of accurate and well-written texts on the history of American education. No point would be served by listing all of them; four, however, deserve special mention because of their high quality and because of the debt I owe them.

The first was written by Ellwood P. Cubberley, who was for many years a professor of education at Leland Stanford Junior University. Entitled *Public Education in the United States: A Study and Interpretation of American Educational History*, it was published in 1910 and revised several times in later years. At one time almost every student who took a course in educational history in the United States read Cubberley's interesting book; it goes without saying that the author reaped substantial royalties from his work. In time, however, Cubberley's book came under criticism, the most telling of which recently was from the pen of Bernard Bailyn in his superb book, *Education in the Forming of American Society* (1960). Cubberley, it was said, emphasized the process of schooling instead of education in its broadest definition and the forces and events that influenced the growth of public schooling in the United States. Another criticism was that Cubberley gave too much credit to the New England states as pacesetters and ignored or treated only superficially educational developments elsewhere. This omission was corrected to some extent by Edgar W. Knight, with the publication in 1929 of his *Education in the United States*. Knight used primary sources, especially in dealing with education in the South.

Another criticism historians have leveled at Cubberley and other writers on educational history is that they tend to see schooling as a desirable end in itself and to bend the facts, when necessary, to make as strong a case as possible for increasing public support of the educational enterprise in the United States. These writers, it has been charged, have not always maintained the disinterest so essential to the serious scholar, but have on occasion allowed the truth to be subverted in the interests of educational reform. Unquestionably there is substance to these charges, especially against writers of a half-century ago; on the other hand, the same charge of prejudice can be leveled against historians of any period, including our own. The question is not whether the writer is biased (all writers are), but whether his bias seriously distorts his ability to gather and interpret evidence.

Despite criticism of Cubberley's remarkable text—one of the first of its kind—the fact remains that it is readable, crammed with facts, and can be found on the shelves of many professional libraries; moreover, it is one of the first sources consulted by even its critics in verifying a statistic or settling an argument on schooling in the United States.

My recommendation of Adolph E. Meyer's *An Educational History of the American People* is threefold. First, I owe it a debt of gratitude; more important, the prose style is lively, and the interpretations of men and measures are always intriguing. Meyer's view of the world is just unique enough to provide his reader with a fresh perspective. To the student interested in educational history one might give this advice: "Yes, it would be wise to attend the lectures, read the regular texts, and examine the documents in the books of readings and documentary history. But whatever you do, don't fail to read Meyer." The final section of this book is a "Bibliographical Note" that provides the student with an invaluable 57 pages of readings and sources.

Another fine text, *A History of Education in American Culture*, by R. Freeman Butts and Lawrence Cremin, overcomes some of the deficiencies of earlier works such as Cubberley's by emphasizing the extent to which education was shaped by social institutions, forces, and trends. Another book that offers both graceful prose and deep insights is *The School in the American Social Order*, by Newton Edwards and Herman G. Richey. These authors, like Butts and Cremin, include a list of references and a section on questions for study and discussion at the end of each chapter.

For the student interested in the general history of American higher education, there are two volumes that complement one another. The first, which appeared in 1958, and was revised in 1968, is the work of John Brubacher and Willis Rudy and is entitled *Higher Education in Transition*. The second, published in 1962 and entitled *The American College and University: A History*, was written by Frederick Rudolph of Williams College. Rudolph's book is delightfully readable and a sound general history, and it contains, moreover, a bibliography which is the best of its kind. The book by Brubacher and Rudy, on the other hand, provides more information on a variety of special topics, and the revised edition affords a lengthy list of college and university histories. Incidentally, some historians reviewing a volume of institutional history will feel compelled to cite the myth that holds all such studies to be incompetent, poor history, and badly written. Anyone who perpetuates this myth has read few of the institutional histories written in the last two decades. Admittedly, some institutional histories have been the work of retired college presidents or professors who have no desire, for example, to see a centennial observance marred by indiscreet disclosures and the raking over of old scandals.

The truth is, however, that as more and more competent historians turn to the writing of institutional histories, we can hope to see a concomitant rise in quality of the works in this field.

Readers interested in developments in higher education since the appearance of Rudolph's book in 1962—surely one of the most turbulent periods in the entire history of higher education—must be satisfied with the plethora of essays and books on such special topics as student unrest and changes in patterns of governance. As yet, no book has appeared that adequately analyzes events of this most recent period. Some would argue that writers are still too close to the unsettling events of the 1960s and 1970s to handle them dispassionately. This may be so; on the other hand, one finds no dearth of polemic.

Anyone interested in primary sources compiled in a documentary history or book of readings will find several titles from which to choose. One of the best is a two-volume work entitled *American Higher Education: A Documentary History*, edited by Richard Hofstadter and Wilson Smith; it contains documents (a bit overweighted, perhaps, by those dealing with academic freedom) and an excellent set of prefatory essays that far exceed their introductory function. One of the most comprehensive books of readings is that edited by Edgar W. Knight and Clifton L. Hall under the title *Readings in American Educational History*. Two other volumes of collected papers, both with excellent commentaries, are David B. Tyack's *Turning Points in American Educational History* and Daniel Calhoun's *The Educating of Americans: A Documentary History*.

The reader interested in those various plans for a national system of education proposed for the early days of the nation will want to examine Frederick Rudolph's *Essays on Education in the Early Republic*. This collection, published in 1965, also includes the plans of Benjamin Rush, Noah Webster, Robert Coram, Simeon Dogget, Samuel Harrison Smith, Amable-Louis-Rose De Lafitte Du Courteil, and Samuel Knox.

In the past few years there has been an increased interest

in the education of American blacks and Indians. *A History of Negro Education in the South* won Henry Allen Bullock the Bancroft Prize for American history in 1968, but unfortunately the author of this excellent book devotes only a few ages to the education of Negroes in the early national period. A book on the education of Indians by Evelyn C. Adams, entitled *American Indian Education: Government Schools and Economic Progress* and published in 1946, is disappointing in its few references to primary sources. Other books that deal with the education of racial minorities include Benjamin Quarles, *The Negro in the Making of America*; Horace Mann Bond's much older book, *The Education of the Negro in the American Social Order* (1934), and Loren Katz's *Eyewitness: The Negro in American Life* (1966). An interesting article by David Tyack in the *History of Education Quarterly* (Fall 1969) includes a sampling of sources on the education of American blacks. In the preparation of this book I am indebted to Mrs. Sharon Campbell for her unpublished manuscript, entitled "Indian and Negro Education: 1776–1830."

Books about old textbooks are plentiful; two of the more engaging being John Alfred Nietz's *Old Textbooks* (1961) and Charles Carpenter's *History of American Schoolbooks* (1963).

The rise of the academy in the United States is given competent treatment in Theodore Sizer's *The Age of the Academies*, a volume in the "Classics in Education Series" published by Teachers College, Columbia University. I describe the national university movement in the United States in *The National University* (1966).

Several guides to research in the history of education are available including Joe Park's *The Rise of American Education: An Annotated Bibliography* (1965), William W. Brickman's *A Guide to Research in Educational History* (1949), and Jurgen Herbst's *The History of American Education* (1973). An indispensable guide to the student of educational thought is Merle Curti's *The Social Ideas of American Educators* (revised 1959).

It goes without saying, however, that to find the richest

sources of all, one must consult state, local, and university historical archives, collections, journals, and the like. Their number is so great that it is pointless to attempt to list them. From time to time, however, the *History of Education Quarterly* has published a listing of the articles that have appeared in the various state historical journals and elsewhere. Special attention should be given to the *Quarterly*'s Volume VII, Number 3, Fall 1967; Volume VII, Number 4, Winter 1968; Volume IX, Number 1, Spring 1969; Volume XII, Number 1, Spring 1972; Volume XII, Number 4, Winter 1972.

Another rich source of information and analysis is to be provided by term papers, master's essays, and doctoral dissertations. Although there is no way to collect all such materials, a careful check of the *Dissertation Abstracts* and other sources will list most theses. A list of many (but not all) dissertations on a particular subject can be obtained through the "Datrix" technique, which enables the student to acquire the titles of as many dissertations on a topic as the Xerox Corporation has in its records in Ann Arbor, Michigan. Success in locating the dissertations relevant to one's field of inquiry will depend on ingenuity in supplying certain key words to be used in a computerized run-through of all dissertation titles on file. Of course, the student may purchase a copy of any dissertation that seems to bear on his scholarly interests.

The following are a sampling of the dissertations that deal with educational matters in the early national period: "Benjamin Rush and the Theory and Practice of Republican Education in Pennsylvania" (James Bonar, The Johns Hopkins University, 1965); "The Social and Political Views of Samuel Harrison Smith" (Seymour Brostoff, New York University 1952); "Influences on Thomas Jefferson's Theory and Practice of Higher Education" (John Carey, the University of Michigan, 1969); "The Concept of Elocution in Common School Readers Used in the United States Between 1820 and 1860" (Laura Chase, University of California-Los Angeles, 1967); "The Educational Philosophy of Thomas Jefferson" (John Densford,

Oklahoma State University, 1961); "The Proper Objects of a Gratuitous Education: The Free School Society of the City of New York, 1805–1826" (Julia Duffy, Columbia University, 1968); "Some Factors Influencing Public Opinion on Free Schools in Pennsylvania: 1880–1835" (John Dwyer, Temple University, 1956); "The Educational Views and Influence of Samuel Knox" (Ashley Foster, New York University, 1952); "Benjamin Franklin as an Educator" (M. Roberta Warf Keiter, University of Maryland, 1957); "A Study to Determine the Factors Responsible for Connecticut's Loss of Leadership in the Common School Movement between 1820–1850" (Bernard McKearney, University of Connecticut, 1966); "The Contribution of William Smith, 1727–1803, to the Development of Higher Education in the United States" (William R. Peters, University of Michigan, 1968); "Benjamin Franklin and His Views and Opinion on Education" (Thomas J. Powers, Michigan State University, 1965); "The Influence and Contribution of Noah Webster Upon Language Arts Teaching in the Nineteenth-Century" (William Rosenberg, University of Connecticut, 1967); "The Contributions of the American Working Man's Movement to the Establishment of Common Schools in New York and Pennsylvania between 1820 and 1842" (Joan Lee Stachiw, Pennsylvania State University, 1963); and "Technology and Educational Reform in Early America" (Thomas K. Shotwell, Louisiana State University, 1965). Finally, mention must be made of the unusual wealth of information afforded by the dissertation, "Education as Revealed by New England Newspapers Prior to 1850" (Vera Butler, Temple University, 1935).

Among the most valuable books on any era are those written either by persons who lived through the events and possessed the ability to record their impressions with vividness and accuracy, or by those who were close enough chronologically to make intelligent use of documents and interviews with their immediate predecessors. In the latter class is the book by the remarkable historian, Henry Adams, author of one of the best autobiographies written by an American. Although Adams knew

New England better than the middle states and the South, his description of the United States at the beginning of the nineteenth century in Volume I of his *History of the United States* and his analysis of the promise and weaknesses of his beloved country rank with the best available.

As interesting and important as the study based on reliable and excellent secondary sources is, nothing delights the scholar more than to come on a literate description and analysis of an event written by an actual eyewitness (unless it be three such independent descriptions of the same event). One such treasure exists in the engrossing account of life in New England and the middle states written by Timothy Dwight, president of Yale College from 1795 to 1817. At the end of term, Dwight delighted in travel through New England and the middle states making notes on what he saw and was told. *Travel in New England and New York* was published in four volumes in 1823 (and recently reissued). Inordinately fond of tales of Indian massacres, Dwight seemed to relish any opportunity to recount some earlier outrage; while he must be taken with more than a grain of salt—he was, moreover, hopelessly chauvinistic—this New England clergyman and college president wrote with a freshness and insight seldom equaled. At his best in his descriptions of the countryside and the activities and attitudes of those he met, Dwight presents the reader with a fascinating contemporary portrait of the best and some of the worst in the early national period.

Another eyewitness record of conditions of the time was also the work of a clergyman, the Reverend Warren Burton, in his warm and for the most part gentle account of his boyhood schooling, *The District School as It Was*, published in 1833.

For an overview of education in its many parts, consider the 161-book collection published by Arno Press under the comprehensive title *American Education: Its Men, Institutions and Ideas*. Lawrence Cremin served as advisory editor of the collection, which deserves in all respects its publisher's claims to provide a basic library of educational thought and practice.

This list would be incomplete without mention of two recent works that are both scholarly and beautifully written. They are Charles Burgess and Merle Borrowman, *What Doctrines to Embrace* (1969), and Jonathan Messerli's biography, *Horace Mann* (1972).

There are so many other books worthy of mention in a brief bibliography such as this. Here are only a few of them. Carl Kaestle, *The Evolution of an Urban School System: New York City 1750–1850* (1973), Henry Cope, *The Evolution of the Sunday School* (1911), Gordon C. Lee, *Crusade Against Ignorance: Thomas Jefferson on Education* (1961), and Donald Tewksbury, *The Founding of American Colleges and Universities Before the Civil War* (1932). The student interested in articles and monographs to be found in periodicals will find one of the several guides to research on the history of education to be most helpful. An excellent such guide is Jurgen Herbst's, *The History of American Education* (1973). Two general American history textbooks that I have found to be both informative and a pleasure to read are Samuel Eliot Morison, *The Oxford History of the American People*, and Henry Bamford Parkes, *The United States of America: A History.*

a chronology: 1776-1831

1776	Signing of the Declaration of Independence
	Phi Beta Kappa society founded at William and Mary College
1777	Liberty Hall Academy chartered in North Carolina
1778	Phillips Andover Academy established in Massachusetts
	A "Treaty of Alliance" signed with France
1779	Thomas Jefferson submitted his proposal entitled a *Bill for the More General Diffusion of Knowledge,* a plan for a school system for Virginia
1780	The American Academy of Arts and Science founded in Boston
1781	General Cornwallis surrendered his army at Yorktown
1782	Gilbert Stuart, the artist, painted his splendid portrait, *The Skater*
	Harvard College added a medical department
1783	Noah Webster published his *Grammatical Institute of the English Language* (The American "blue-back" Spelling Book)

	The "Treaty of Paris" ended the war with Great Britain
1784	Judge Tapping Reeve opened his law school in Litchfield, Connecticut
	The Regents of the University of the State of New York were authorized to organize schools and colleges for the state
	Jedidiah Morse published *Geography Made Easy*, the first American geography schoolbook
	A daily newspaper, *The Pennsylvania Packet and Daily Advertiser*, began publication
1785	Enactment of the Land Ordinance of 1785, which set aside the sixteenth section of each township in the Northwest Territory for the support of education
1786	Benjamin Rush proposed the establishment of a national university
	The *Pittsburgh Gazette* began publication
1786–1787	"Daniel Shay's Rebellion"
1786–1794	John Trumbull painted his conception of the signing of the "Declaration of Independence"
1787	The Northwest Land Ordinance declared that "schools and the means of education shall be forever encouraged." Another ordinance that same year set aside "two complete townships to be given perpetually for the purpose of a university...."
	The Constitutional Convention met in Philadelphia
	The "Free African Society" was founded in Philadelphia to provide elementary schooling for the children of Negroes
	The Contrast, a play by Royall Tyler, was performed in New York
	John Fitch launched his first steamboat on the Delaware River
	York Academy was founded in York, Pennsylvania
1789	George Washington elected first president of the United States

The University of North Carolina was chartered
(The first classes met in 1795)

A Massachusetts law added the study of English,
arithmetic, orthography, and "decent behavior" to
the traditionally required school studies of reading
and writing

A novel entitled *Power of Sympathy*, by William
Hill Brown, was published

1790   Jacob Perkins invented a nail-making machine

1791   Ten Amendments (the Bill of Rights) were added to
the Constitution

First "Bank of the United States" opened in
Philadelphia

1792   George Washington was reelected without
opposition

Joel Barlow's book, *Advice to the Privileged
Orders* . . . , was published in London

1793   Wars of the French Revolution began. George
Washington issued a proclamation of American
neutrality

Williams College chartered

Eli Whitney invented the cotton gin

The [Old] Farmer's Almanac published by
Robert B. Thomas

1794   The "Whiskey Rebellion"

Thomas Paine's *Age of Reason* appeared in America

A turnpike opened between Lancaster and
Philadelphia, Pennsylvania

1795   Union College was chartered in Schenectady,
New York

The "Treaty of Greenville" brought 15 years of
comparative peace with the Indians in the Northwest Territory

"Jay's Treaty" signed with Great Britain

1796   Pinckney's Treaty with Spain

John Adams elected President over Thomas
Jefferson

1797	Samuel Knox and Samuel Smith shared a prize awarded by the American Philosophical Society for the best plan for a national system of education
1797–1798	American commissioners to France were insulted
1798	Passage of the Alien and Sedition Acts
	Undeclared naval war with France
	Wieland: Or The Transformation, a novel by Charles Brockden Brown
1798–1799	Virginia and Kentucky "Resolutions"
1799	Death of George Washington
1800	Convention of 1800 resolving many differences with France
	Thomas Jefferson elected president over John Adams
	Gabriel, a slave, led a brief uprising in Virginia
1801	A newspaper, *The Evening Post*, was published in New York
	A magazine, the *Philadelphia Port Folio*, was begun
	The University of Georgia opened
1802	The United States Military Academy at West Point was founded
1803	William Ellery Channing, a Unitarian, took the pulpit of the Federal Street Church in Boston
	The Louisiana Purchase
	Marbury versus Madison. The Supreme Court declared a law of Congress unconstitutional
1804	The architect, Benjamin Latrobe, built the first building at Dickinson College in Pennsylvania
	Thomas Jefferson reelected president over Charles C. Pinckney
1804–1806	The Lewis and Clark expedition reached the Pacific Ocean traveling by land and river over much of the northern Louisiana Purchase Territory
1805	Johann Pestalozzi opened a teacher's training institute in Switzerland
	Methodism claimed 6000 new converts
	A Free School Society formed in New York

1805–1807	American ships seized under Napoleon's Decrees and British Orders in Council
1806	"Lancastrian System" introduced in the United States
1807	The "Chesapeake-Leopard Affair"
	Embargo Acts
	Robert Fulton's steamboat, "Clermont," sailed on the Hudson River as a commercial success
1808	James Madison elected president over Charles C. Pinckney
	The foreign slave trade was declared illegal
1809	Washington Irving wrote *A History of New York*
	The Nonintercourse Act replaced the Embargo Acts
1811	Battle of Tippecanoe
1812	James Madison reelected president over DeWitt Clinton
	John Stevens published *Documents Tending to Prove the Superiority of Rail-Ways and Steam Carriages over Canal Navigation*
	American Antiquarian Society organized in Worcester, Massachusetts
	Gideon Hawley of New York appointed first state superintendent of Schools
1812–1815	War of 1812
1814–1815	Treaty of Ghent ended the War of 1812
1815	Boston Handel and Haydn Society formed
	American Education Society created to provide funds for student aid
	North American Review published
	Cotton exports are double the value of next most important crop, tobacco
1816	James Monroe elected over Rufus King
1817	Second "Bank of the United States" chartered
	Andrew Jackson invaded Spanish Florida
	Thomas Hopkins Gallaudet opened school for the deaf in Hartford, Connecticut
1817–1825	Erie Canal was built

1818	Convention of 1818 resolved many differences with Great Britain
	National Road reached the Ohio River
	Virginia Commissioners, including Thomas Jefferson, met in Rockfish Gap to recommend a university for the state
1819	Washington Allston painted *Moonlit Landscape*
	William Ellery Channing laid down principles of Unitarianism
	Dartmouth College versus Woodward protected private college charters against undue legislative interference
	McCulloch versus Maryland. The Supreme Court upheld the constitutionality of the "Bank of the United States"
	Depression
1819–1821	Treaty with Spain secured Florida for the United States
1820	James Monroe reelected without opposition
	Land prices reduced by the Land Act of 1820
	Missouri Compromise
	Musical Fund Society of Philadelphia was founded
1821	"English Classical School" (later referred to as the English High School) opened in Boston
	Emma Willard opened her Troy Female Seminary
1822	Denmark Vesey, a free black, led a brief uprising
	Samuel F. B. Morse painted *The Old House of Representatives*
1822–1825	Thomas Jefferson designed the buildings for the University of Virginia
1823	Monroe Doctrine proclaimed
	"Great Rebellion" at Harvard. Out of a class of 70, 43 seniors were expelled
1824	Rensselaer Polytechnic Institute founded
	Tariff of 1824, a high protective tariff
	John Quincy Adams elected over Andrew Jackson and others

Charles Grandison Finney became a Presbyterian and began his career as an itinerant evangelist

1825   University of Virginia opened

1826   James Fenimore Cooper wrote *The Last of the Mohicans*

Josiah Holbrook organized American lyceum (adult education)

1827   Society for the Promotion of Public Schools was founded in Philadelphia

Massachusetts law for secondary schools passed

John Neagle painted *Pat Lyon at the Forge*

Samuel Griswold Goodrich began publishing the "Peter Parley" textbooks

1828   Andrew Jackson elected president over John Quincy Adams

"Tariff of Abominations"

Yale Report defended the collegiate curricular status quo

1829   James Smithson's will left property to the United States to be used to found an institution to advance knowledge. In 1846 the Smithsonian Institution was created

1830   First railway passengers carried in the United States by horse-drawn cars

1831   Nat Turner, a slave, led a brief uprising in Virginia

Cyrus H. McCormick tested his reaper near Steele's Tavern, Virginia

index